CREATIVE WRITING

A Practical Guide

Julia Casterton

**MACMILLAN
EDUCATION**

First published 1986
Reprinted 1988

Published by
MACMILLAN EDUCATION LTD
Houndmills, Basingstoke, Hampshire RG21 2XS
and London
Companies and representatives
throughout the world

Typeset by Wessex Typesetters
(Division of The Eastern Press Ltd)
Frome, Somerset

Printed in Hong Kong

British Library Cataloguing in Publication Data
Casterton, Julia
Creative writing: a practical guide.
1. Creative writing
I. Title
808'.042   PN 193
ISBN 0-333-37863-6

Contents

Acknowledgements

I want to thank Maria McKay, Antoinette Vass, Nigel Young and Rick Stanwood, who helped me with different parts of my life, from childcare to companionship, while I wrote this book, and Tina Betts, who discussed the work of literary agents with me.

The author and publishers wish to thank the following who have kindly given permission for the use of copyright material: Jonathan Cape Ltd for extract from 'Spelling' from *True Stories* by Margaret Atwood (1982); Lawrence Pollinger Ltd on behalf of the estate of Mrs Frieda Lawrence Ravagli for 'The Oxford Voice' from *Selected Poems* by D. H. Lawrence

Preface

I have written this book for people who want to write, who know there is a writer inside them, but who find the leap of taking themselves seriously, and so beginning to write every day, an all but impossible one to take. Equally, it is for those who have written but are now silent. If you are a writer (and if you are there is a kind of death in not writing) you have to make many new beginnings – because of all the things in your life that can make you, for a time, lose your tongue. I hope this book will encourage those who have been silenced to hear again their own writer's voice: to take the risk of beginning again.

This book is dedicated to Hester Stanwood, the gift of a woman to her daughter, that she may never lose her tongue.

1
Why Write?

I often wonder why I write. I've spent hours talking to friends, writers and non-writers about it. For the first 25 years of my life I was convinced that everybody was either writing or wanted to write a novel. Finally a woman I worked with told me in no uncertain terms that *she* had no such desire, which threw me utterly. I'd assumed she was writing in secret, as I was – pursuing a universal dirty habit that demanded solitude and a quiet place – when instead she was watching TV or out at the pub with friends: being social. Writing isn't usually a social activity, except when you're working on exercises together in a writers' group – and even then you'll find that you do most of your writing alone, in whatever space and time you can carve out for yourself.

One thing seems clear: it isn't as natural as breathing. The myth of the 'natural' writer, who spins vast, architectural webs of exalted verse or prose is a treacherous lie which many writers have done their best to rub out, only to watch it appear again, healthy as ever, in literary columns, popular films about literary 'giants', even in the biographies of writers. No matter how much writers protest, non-writers seem to like the idea that writing is easy, not the arduous manual, emotional and intellectual labour writers know it to be. Simone de Beauvoir expressed great irritation when someone implied that anyone could have written *The Memoirs of a Dutiful Daughter*. If anyone could have written it, why was she the only one to have done so? Writers constantly have to deal with this prejudice, and it is well worth remembering this before discussing writing with casual acquaintances.

I think people write because they need to. Lawrence Durrell described it as a way of becoming more human. This process can take the form of fly-fishing with some people, Japanese boxing or embroidery with others. With writers it takes the form of writing. It takes time to understand this need, but I believe that the more we write, the more fully we grasp why it is we want to, have to. In *A Room of One's Own* Virginia Woolf argues that even though a person's gift for writing may be small, it is nevertheless death to hide it. The writer, for whatever reasons, is compelled to write. She or he may be able to suppress the compulsion for months or even years, believing perhaps that there are more worthwhile, less selfish ways to spend one's time. But who can tell the damage we do to our writing voices when we roughly silence them for long stretches?

There is a magic in words. We wade around in so many glossy pointless circulars, so many yards of dubious newsprint, that it is easy to forget this primary fact: it is words, and our ability to speak and write, which make us human. Words give us power over every other creature and thing in the natural world. Those who cannot write have less power than those who can: their acts of naming are restricted to those who will listen to them, those in the immediate locality. They cannot easily communicate with other societies or with those who are not yet born, as people can who know how to write. Bertolt Brecht advises people who are hungry to learn the alphabet. Knowledge of the skills of literacy is an important step towards taking control of one's own life.

Many societies, our own included, have imposed severe penalties on those who have aspired to the power that writing can give. Ruling groups have found that their interests are best safeguarded if they are supported by a work force which cannot think for itself in the coherent way writing affords. The agents of the Spanish Inquisition burned books, as did the Nazis. Books can be dangerous because the reading and writing of them involves us in an exercise of intellectual freedom.

Imaginative writings, whether poetry, fiction or plays, create another place for the reader to inhabit, offer an alternative world which may challenge the real one. They are, in the most fundamental sense, magical: they weave spells, they conjure something out of nothing. William Shakespeare writes:

The poet's eye, in a fine frenzy rolling,
Doth glance from heaven to earth, from earth to heaven;
And as imagination bodies forth
The forms of things unknown, the poet's pen
Turns them into shapes, and gives to airy nothing
A local habitation and a name.
                    A Midsummer Night's Dream, V.i.

and Margaret Atwood, in a poem called 'Spelling', writes:

My daughter plays on the floor
with plastic letters,
red, blue and hard yellow,
learning how to spell,
spelling,
how to make spells.

And I wonder how many women
denied themselves daughters,
closed themselves in rooms,
drew the curtains
so they could mainline words.

A word after a word
after a word is power.

Shakespeare and Atwood seem to have different attitudes towards this magic. Shakespeare's poet is in a frenzy, possessed by the spirit of artistic creation. No sooner has he imagined something than his pen transforms imagination into characters on the page. It all sounds spontaneous, unconscious and . . . easy. Atwood's daughter, on the other hand, and the women poets she imagines are doing something different with words. The daughter is *playing* with letters and *learning* how to spell. The women are shutting themselves off, choosing the high that comes from writing instead of accepting their place as bearers and nurturers of children. They are in conflict with what is expected of them. They don't imagine they can have their cake and eat it too.

Women, men and writing

Women and men stand in a different relationship to language and women writers should remember this fact both while they are writing and when they receive rejection slips from publishers. To begin with, young girls and women are frequently told that they talk too much, that they make facile use of words, that they chatter idly. Talking is something they do easily but not well, it is said. It is also said that girls are more verbally adept and can express complex concepts more readily than boys. I think it is the critical statements, rather than the words of praise, that are more often uttered in the hearing of girls. For a girl to take up her pen at all, then, is an act of great self-assertion. She is expressing herself against the popular wisdom concerning her sex.

Far fewer articles in magazines are written by women than men. Why is this? Did something terrible happen to those verbally adept young girls as they grew older? Did they lose the pleasure of saying what they wanted to say? Or are they grown up and still writing but to no avail? Does no one want to read their work? Are the subjects they write about simply not engaging to the editors of these magazines? How many of the editors are women? These are questions that women writers have to ask, questions we cannot escape from.

Things are changing though. In Britain, we now have three publishing houses committed to women's writing and at least two of the large publishing companies now carry a separate list for books of special interest to women. This is great news for the new generation of women writers, but for some it is already too late. They have lost heart, stashed away their manuscripts and told themselves they were never really writers anyway.

However, that isn't to say that male writers have it easy. Finding a publisher is hard for all writers and we know from the letters and diaries of writers as important as Gerard Manley Hopkins, Joseph Conrad and Hermann Melville how painful it is when the writing will not come. But I do believe that women experience another, relentless denial of their powers, which begins as soon as they can speak, if not before, and makes the act of writing for them primarily an act of rebellion.

Writing and conflict

Conflict and rebellion can perform a creative part in the formation of the writer when we learn how to use them. It is through the written word that the writer asserts the *difference* between herself or himself and other people and other writers. Philip Larkin (in *Required Writing*) said that part of the reason he wrote was that no one else had written what he wanted to read, and W. B. Yeats claimed that rhetoric emerges out of one's quarrel with other people and poetry out of the quarrel with oneself. The quarrels and conflicts we have buried within us also possess a rich fecundating power for the writer.

Think of your own favourite writer, of all the books she or he has written. Do you find knots of conflict that the writer keeps trying to unravel and then tie up again? Do you find that, as Adrienne Rich wrote of Marie Curie, 'her wounds came from the same source as her power?'

Spilling the knots from one's entrails out onto paper isn't likely to make a poem or story that others will want to read, but many writers do have to go through the 'spilling' process in order to know just what it is they have to hammer into shape. Words come out differently on paper to how we imagine them in our heads. We discover ourselves through the form of the sentence. The act of transforming our knots into marks on the paper begins to give a discipline. Something inside says 'You can't say it that way, it doesn't work' and so we change it. Even as we start to write, we find ourselves making contact with feelings for rhythm and style. Later we will revise the writing more stringently: pruning, shifting the weight, reordering, until every part holds every other part and it *stands*: it means what we want it to mean.

Getting ready to write

In his book *A Separate Reality*, Carlos Casteneda explores the importance of what he calls 'finding your spot' before you can begin to learn anything. Finding a place for one's writing work, both a practical place – a room in the house, a desk, a table, a comfortable chair – and a place in one's imagination are crucial prerequisites for enabling the writing voice to grow and develop. The writing self has to be nurtured. Remember that your chair is important. Just as you cannot live easily under a leaking roof, so you cannot write easily on a chair that is not right for you. Think about the light that is cast on your paper. Is it bright enough? Does it illuminate what you are doing properly? Think too about your paper. Colette bought well-finished paper that her pen could flow across easily. These things are not trivial. They are the material conditions of a writer's life, and they affect your writing.

When we first experience the desire to write, our writing voice may well be timid, weak, needy and underfed, so we need to feed it, to let the writer-self know that it is significant for us. We need to purposefully put time aside to spend with it, listen to it. The writer in us has to know that we are making it a priority, that we are prepared to let other obligations go in order to play with it, nourish it, accord it a central place in our lives. If, when I describe the writer-self, it sounds as though I am describing a baby, that is entirely intentional.

When you are getting ready to write, think carefully about what you need, about what will nourish the starveling child. Writing time is *your* time; you need to claim it for yourself, often against the demands of other people. Sometimes this may feel like a military strategy and it is quite in order to treat it this way: to plot and plan to take the fortress which is your imaginary castle, your silent, fertile abode, despite the background of your everyday tasks and obligations. When you begin to feel guilty, remind yourself that it's for the child's sake.

You may need to ask yourself questions like 'When am I likely to have some space to myself?', 'When is it likely to be quiet?', 'Do I need to leave the house or can I find time at home, when the others are out?', 'Can I work when there are other people around?'. I find it wise to let people know that I am writing, that I need solitude. Others *do* learn to respect your need to be alone, if you persist in maintaining it. Remember that if you take this need seriously, others will come to accept it.

Opening the storehouse door

This is the first exercise in this book and in certain ways the most important. It constitutes your attempt to explore your writer-self, to find out its needs, its insecurities and its strengths. The aim of the exercise is to begin to discover why you relate to written language in the way you do and to trigger the first probings into your own, unique way of understanding yourself and your world. Ask yourself these questions:

What are my earliest memories of speaking and writing?
Whom do I remember talking to most as a child?
Was it primarily a relationship of conflict or harmony?
What do I remember about learning to write?
What were the words I was not allowed to say?

Do I have an early memory of *misunderstanding*, when something I said was misunderstood, perhaps with painful or embarrassing consequences, by a friend, a member of my family or a teacher?

With whom did I feel most open and confident about expressing myself in words?

Was there a difference between what I felt I could *say* and what I felt I could *write*?

These are hard questions to answer, so be prepared to take your time and dig deep. It's not a race or a competition, but a process of discovering, or uncovering, your own writing voice. Note down the first thoughts that come into your head and follow where they lead; but do try to answer all the questions.

When you've made the notes, structure them into two or three pages of narrative prose. Even if you want to make a poem in the end, write in prose first, just to make sure you're clear about the feelings and experiences that have come to the surface. Yeats wrote out his poems in prose first: it is a discipline which works. The whole exercise, from beginning to end, should take about two hours, with plenty of time at the start just for thinking. Be prepared to *centre* yourself in revery, to give yourself up to your memories just as your sleeping self gives itself up to a dream. Try to protect yourself from interruptions – but if an interruption is unavoidable, don't worry. Do what you have to do, but keep the memories with you, let them take root in your conscious mind while you're away from your desk. Interruptions are not always a curse; I sometimes find that a lost association breaks the surface for air precisely when I've stopped actively thinking about the writing. When you've made a physical space – a table and a chair – for your writer-self, you will find that an inner space begins to open up in the imagination. You will learn to hold your work with you even when you are prevented from doing it. Alexander Solzhenitsyn held much of his work in his mind while he was in a labour camp. He stored it up – the mind's ability to store is inexhaustible – and wrote it down when he was finally released. If *that* is possible, then you can certainly get through interruptions without fear of losing your load.

When you've finished writing, put it away for two or three days: leave it, don't look at it for a while. You are of course free to write anything else while you leave your first piece fallow. But while you have separated yourself from your own autobiographical work, take a look at the following extracts:

> She developed a method in her whippings: standing with her switch in her hand, she would order me to come before her. I would plead or cry or run away. But at last I had to come. Without taking hold of me, she forced me to stand in one spot of my own will, while she whipped me on all sides. Afterwards, when I continued to sob as children do, she would order me to stop or she would 'stomp me into the ground'. I remember once that I could not and with one swoop she was upon me – over the head, down the back, on my bare legs, until in agony and terror I ran for the house screaming for my father. Yet what could I say to my father – I was little and could not explain. And he would not believe.
>
> My mother continued to say that I lied. But I did not know it. I was never clear. What was truth and what was fancy I could not know. To me, the wind in the tree tops really carried stories on its back; the red bird that came to our cherry tree told me things; the fat, velvety flowers in the forest laughed and I answered; the little calf in the field held long conversations with me.
>
> But at last I learned to know what a lie was: to induce my mother to stop beating me I would lie – I would say, yes, I

had lied and was sorry, and then she would whip me for
having withheld the admission so long. As time went on, to
avoid a whipping, I learned to tell her only the things I
thought she wanted to hear.

'I have but one child who is stubborn and a liar, and that is
Marie,' she would tell strangers or neighbours. At first I was
humiliated to tears; later I became hardened; later still I
accepted it as a fact and did not even try to deny it.

It has been one of the greatest struggles of my life to learn
to tell the truth. . . .

Agnes Smedley, *Daughter of Earth*.

Remind me how we loved our mother's body
our mouths drawing the first
thin sweetness from her nipples

our faces dreaming hour on hour
in the salt smell of her lap. Remind me
how her touch melted childgrief

how she floated great and tender in our dark
or stood guard over us
against our willing

and how we thought she loved
the strange male body first
that took, that took, whose taking seemed a law

and how she sent us weeping
into that law
how we remet her in our childbirth visions

erect, enthroned, above
a spiral stair
and crawled and panted toward her

I know, I remember, but
hold me, remind me
of how her woman's flesh was made taboo to us

Adrienne Rich, 'Sibling Mysteries' in
The Dream of a Common Language.

Both writers explore an early relationship, the conflict and misunderstanding within it and the terrible sense of loss which arises when one is deprived, in one sense or another, of one's mother. Agnes Smedley's heroine, Marie, talks about having to shut her mother out, shut off from her, in order to protect herself against her mother's extraordinary cruelty – while Adrienne Rich works on the feeling of severance, of being deprived of her mother in a culture which insists that the daughters turn away from the mother toward the father.

Your early experiences form a rich vein – the mother lode perhaps – from which you can learn to dig your finest material. What you do with it once you've brought it to the surface is another matter: it is enough for now that you acknowledge it is there and begin to discover ways of getting at it.

Your notebook

I think you will have found that this exercise produced more thoughts, images and ideas than you were able to use in what you finally wrote. Do not throw any of them away: writers make new garments out of castoffs all the time. Transfer all the thoughts and images you like into a notebook. The superflux will provide new material for you whenever ideas are not coming easily. Your notebook should be small enough to fit in your bag or pocket and have covers which are firm enough to prevent it from being damaged easily. Record in it anything you fancy: a new word, a new way of describing a colour, a particular action you saw performed which you'd like to describe in detail while it's fresh.

Your notebook is the tool which enables you to take any experience, any observation, any physical sensation and turn it into something which can be shared by others. In Anna Akhmatova's words, it forms a way of 'bearing witness to the common lot'. Every society requires its witnesses: those who are not afraid to render and preserve in words the range and scope of human experience for that time and that place. When Akhmatova stood in line for 17 months outside the gaol in Leningrad, waiting for news of her son, a woman, hearing her name, approached her and said 'Can you describe this?' to which the poet returned: 'I can.' That woman *needed* the poet; a poem had to be written to ensure that her suffering, and that of numberless others, should not be dishonoured by silence. Writing is a way of honouring the world we live in, its living and its dead.

Writing with the whole self

New writers often say 'Well, I'm writing now. I've started. But when I look at what I've written, I feel it's not all there. There's a dimension missing, it has no depth.' I believe that the reason for this being such a common problem is that we live, in the Western industrialised world, in such a disembodied way. Half the time we carry on as if we didn't have a body: and we only think about our bodies if they trouble us – if we're hungry or in pain. When we are writing we must unlearn this disembodiedness if our work is to achieve the depth and richness we desire: we must learn to speak with our whole body and not just through our mind's eye. The eye is, after all, the most cerebral, least sensuous organ. If we wrote through our eyes alone, we would represent a silent world without smells, without tastes, without texture. I think you will find as you begin to write through *all* your senses, that your writing transforms itself into something more fully alive.

Do this next exercise and then try to *hold* all your senses in listening expectancy in your future writing. The exercise lasts for five days.

On the first day, concentrate only on your sense of touch. Think through your fingers, think through your skin. Be aware of every object, every texture, every current of air your body comes into contact with. Make the surface of your body alive to every stimulation, whether pleasant or not. Then, at the end of the day, write about five hundred words through your sense of touch. Hold onto all you have experienced in the day through your writing: write about everything you have touched.

On the second day, think through your sense of taste. As well as the obvious, known tastes of food and drink, stick your tongue out to discover what the air tastes like. Does rain have a taste? What does leather taste like – and the bricks of a house?

Don't eat anything dangerous – but try to extend the range of things you know the taste of. In the evening, write about them.

On the third day, make your nose into your organ of chief intelligence. Imagine that you are a dog. What can you discover from the smells around you? Follow your nose – to explore the smells you cherish. What do you love to smell? What repels you? Hold onto all these smells until the evening, when you can deliver them up onto the blank paper.

Devote your fourth day to the sense of hearing. Don't worry about what people say, only about the tones of their voices, their cough, their indrawings of breath. Hear the road drill, the articulated lorry, the siren – really hear them. Don't shut them out as you normally do. And then – what do you love to hear? Why are your *beloved* sounds sweet to you? Again, write it all down at the end of the day.

Finally we come to sight, the most human of senses, the one which normally eclipses all the others. Look at movement – the movement of a walking body; look at colour, at light and its shifting patterns. Look at darkness. Look at everything. Then put it on paper in the evening.

Simile and metaphor

In the exercise above, you were probably using simile and metaphor without realising it. It will be useful to you to make your use of them conscious, primarily to avoid cliché, the worm in every writer's bud.

A simile is introduced by a word such as *like*, *as* or *such*. It forms a way of enriching description by comparing one thing with another. For example:

My heart is like a singing bird.

Christina Rosetti

The word metaphor comes from the Greek *metaphorá*, which means transference or 'to carry over'. It occurs when a writer applies a name or a descriptive term to an object to which it is not literally applicable; when a word is carried over from its normal use to a new use. For example:

Boys and girls tumbling in the street, and
playing, were moving jewels.

Thomas Traherne

They weren't literally jewels but because of the flash and
sparkle of their bodies they were metaphorically so.

Simile and metaphor, then, serve to form a bridge between
the experience a writer wants to convey and the reader's own
experience. Christina Rosetti wanted to convey a particular
feeling of overwhelming joy. She did not say 'I feel
overwhelming joy' but 'My heart is like a singing bird' which is
infinitely more powerful. And why? I think because
'overwhelming joy' describes the experience in abstract terms.
We know vaguely what she means, but we do not feel it for
ourselves. We all know, though, how a singing bird makes us
feel and we can imagine how the bird feels as it throws its song
out into the air. Similarly with metaphor. Traherne does not
write 'Boys and girls tumbling in the street, and playing,
flashed this way and that, causing many reflecting lights which
dazzled me'. That is just confusing. He forces us to conjure up
something we can picture entirely for ourselves: the wild
interplay of sparkling colours, shocking and pleasing, that
occurs when jewels move. Both Rosetti and Traherne, through
simile and metaphor, make the reader work harder. They
compel the reader to give something of herself or himself to the
text. It is this work, performed by the writer *and* reader, which
ensures that the communication of feeling can take place.

At this point you should go through the exercise on the senses
and underline where you have used either a simile or a
metaphor. Write all your metaphors and similes down on a
separate sheet of paper. The next stage is an important one in
your ability to evaluate, assess and improve your own work. Go
through each simile and each metaphor in turn and ask
yourself: 'Have I heard this before? Is it too familiar, is it worn
out? Or is it new?' If it is new and unfamiliar, you might
experience a sense of physical pleasure. When I come across a
new metaphor, one that stretches my understanding, I feel
cold. I know that something new has happened, that I've been
forced to make a connection I've never made before. If the
simile or metaphor leaves you feeling exactly the same, if it

doesn't move you, then you could improve it. Work now on making this aspect of your writing stronger, stranger, less expected. One word of warning. Your writing will become ridiculous if you cram metaphors together. Metaphors produce a clear effect on the reader but that effect will become confused and diminished if you use too many or if you mix them up, as in these lamentable examples:

She is a budding star who already sings with a master hand.

and

I smell a rat in the air: I shall nip it in the bud.

Consolidation

An enormous progress will have occurred over the course of these exercises – a progress which you should be aware of, feel and throughly take in. Look again at your first piece of writing. From that you began to make contact with the memories of conflict and strong feeling that will be invaluable in your future writing work. Then look at the five-day exercise on the senses: this has enabled you to start writing with the knowledge you derive from your whole body, rather than merely the abstract, visual knowledge you adduce through your eyes. It has caused you to discover for yourself Margaret Atwood's definition of metaphor:

when . . .
        . . . the word
splits & doubles & speaks
the truth & and body
itself becomes a mouth.

'Spelling'

2
The Space We Inhabit

IN this chapter I want to search with you for the spirit of place, to conjure up the spirit that will give life and breath to descriptions of places. I find that many new writers' stories and poems seem to occur in a spatial and social vacuum: the writer launches straight into an account of action, ideas, thoughts, feelings, without giving any clear sense of where all this is taking place. The result is that the reader feels lost – because the writer hasn't bothered to say where they are. It is frustrating, confusing and severely diminishes the pleasure the writing could bring. But if the place is *there*, living and breathing *through* what happens, then the writing achieves another dimension: it becomes more real.

> The present breaks our hearts. We lie and freeze,
> our fingers icy as a bunch of keys.
> Nothing will thaw these bones except
> memory like an ancient blanket wrapped
> about us when we sleep at home again,
> smelling of picnics, closets, sicknesses,
> old nightmare,
> and insomnia's spreading stain.
> Adrienne Rich, 'Readings of
> History'.

Even poetry, which seems to arise out of nowhere, requires its nest, its squatting place. Look at the image Adrienne Rich has used in her poem: that of home. She conjures up a place to balance against the freezing and breaking of the present. She appeals to our memory of shelter, our perpetual desire for it and fires our memory into longing with the ignition of 'blanket', 'picnics', 'sicknesses' and 'spreading stain'. How much is evoked by spreading stain! A glass of juice toppled onto a white tablecloth; blood dripping onto the carpet or linoleum; the *staining* of childhood by what we learn to fear. We can each supply our own particulars but the important point is that Rich has set us going with her place – her place that grows out of memory.

Now bring your own memories to bear. Clamber back in your mind to the house that meant most to you when you were small. I am going to offer you certain words: *threshold, attic, cellar, kitchen, bedroom, corridor*. Choose one or two of them. Take a blank sheet of paper and write down everything that occurs to you about the word(s) you have chosen, giving yourself about ten minutes.

Were you surprised at how much these words evoked for you, at the richness of feeling and detail they seemed to compel? This was the reason I asked you to return to the house of your childhood: because the places we have loved – or hated – as children remain in the mind as almost a structuring force. They become part of us, both consciously and unconsciously, determining our perceptions and our understanding. When we return to them with the scrutiny of our adult minds, they appear as towering shelters, full of colour and minutely-remembered detail.

When the house of childhood does not serve as a place of support and nurture, when there is intense conflict between different members of the household, then we may find that many memories of *indoors* have been suppressed. If this is true in your own case, try a word like *window, garden* or *playground*. There may have been so much conflict indoors that you had to construct your shelter elsewhere. If, however, you can consciously remember conflicts or tensions inside the house, then go ahead with your writing work. Ask yourself: did conflict regularly occur in certain areas – at the kitchen table for example? I want you to concentrate on the way the rooms themselves bring about certain kinds of behaviour.

A note on ambiguity

You are likely to find that your memories of the house of childhood are split – into fear and security, fire and ice, harmony and conflict. Try to hold these contradictory memories together: don't give in to the temptation to simplify your experience by discarding one important aspect of it. You will find that your writing becomes thinner, poorer, less convincing if you take this easy way out. The courage to hold contradictory impressions together is a brave skill, highly prized by writers. John Keats called it 'negative capability' and it is akin to Ernest Hemingway's 'becoming strong in the broken places'. Michel de Montaigne was so convinced of the importance of contradictoriness that he had emblazoned on the domed ceiling of his library the motto: 'To Every Reason an Equal Reason can be opposed'. So do not be afraid to hold on to impressions that logically seem to cancel one another out.

At first you may have to represent this contradictoriness chronologically, in the manner of 'At first the corridor frightened me, but later I came to love it, its hatpegs, its long coats to hide behind.' With further practice you will discover words that hold more than one meaning, that are themselves ambiguous, enabling you to represent contending realities at a single stroke. Here is an example from *Antony and Cleopatra*, where Cleopatra is persuading the snake to bite and kill her:

Come, thou mortal wretch,
With thy sharp teeth this knot intrinsicate
Of life at once untie. Poor venomous fool,
Be angry, and dispatch.

Act V, Scene ii.

The ambiguous words here are *mortal*, *intrinsicate* and *dispatch*. *Mortal* means both that the snake is mortal, will have a life and then die, and also that it is capable of dealing a mortal blow, of killing. *Intrinsicate* is a deliberately created ambiguity, a made-up word designed to contain two words: intricate and intrinsic. Shakespeare uses it to make us feel how complex and deeply inward is the knot of life, the knot which, while it remains tied, causes Cleopatra to be alive rather than dead. The snake will untie the intricate knot and the deeply-hidden force of life within Cleopatra will cease. *Dispatch* contains the sense of 'to get on with something', haste, and also 'to do away with', to polish off, to send off to the next life.

Be aware of the ambiguities in your own writing. When, reading over your work, you discover one, ask yourself whether or not you intended it. Does it add another dimension? Or is it merely vague? There is a great divide between ambiguity and vagueness. Think how irritated you would be if you began reading a story with the opening sentence 'They were cooking apples.' Does the 'they' refer to the apples or the cooks? It is an unnecessary vagueness that demands clarification. When you question yourself about whether a phrase is ambiguous or vague, the litmus-test is usually 'Did I intend it be written that way? Does that phrase need to be ambiguous?'

Living room, writing room

How can you use your descriptions of place – a room, a garden bench, the large cupboard under the stairs, a lift in a block of flats – to create a mood strong enough to sustain your story? For events do not take place spontaneously, out of nowhere; they come to fullness as a result of many active forces. And the place is not simply the background or backdrop against which the action occurs; it plays its part in the drama.

Look at this description of a place and try to guess some of the action of the story from it.

They arrive at the empty basement flat just after one. She dumps the baby straight into his cot. He is wet and hungry, but also tired. And so is she. They cry themselves to sleep, he behind his wooden bars and she on the big sagging bed. The peeling wallpaper, damp-stained and stinking of mould, decorates her dreams. She awakes to the sight of mildew spreading beneath the window-sill. The odour of must and the small waking cry of a child seep into the air.

Sandra Warne, 'All in a Row'.

I think you will agree that the physical scene determines the atmosphere of the writing, which in its turn determines what will happen, the action of the story. I am making a very simple point: that the material conditions of our lives and of our characters' lives shape, to a large extent, the way those lives

progress. We know this from experience; it seems so obvious
that it is not even worth saying. But if we omit those material
conditions from our writing, then the writing voice loses much
of its authority and power. The reader senses that one large
cause of events is missing.

Spend some time considering the effect of your own living
conditions upon your writing. Under what circumstances do
you write most easily? What prevents you from writing?
Consider too the circumstances of Jane Austen, whose novels
breathe such grace and balance that we assume she wrote with
no distractions:

> 'How she was able to effect all this', her nephew writes in his
> Memoir, 'is surprising, for she had no separate study to
> repair to, and most of the work must have been done in the
> general sitting-room, subject to all kinds of casual
> interruptions. She was careful that her occupation should
> not be suspected by servants or visitors or any persons
> beyond her own family party.'
>
> J. E. Austen, *Memoir of Jane Austen.*

Though the nephew may have exaggerated his aunt's powers of
concentration – Lizzie and Jane in *Pride and Prejudice* each have
a room of their own and servants to build a fire for them – there
is no doubt that our working conditions do influence the quality
of our writing. The place, in this too, plays its part.

Conjuring up the spirit of place

Imagine yourself in a room you love. Close your eyes so you can
walk into it. In revery, walk around your room. Cast your eyes
around slowly; dwell on each object. Imagine yourself picking
one or two of these objects up. How do they feel next to your
skin? How do they smell? Allow yourself to become open and
spongy, soak up the atmosphere and objects in the room until
you feel drenched by them.

This room might exist in your house or flat or only in your
imagination. But whether it is real or imaginary, it should be
something of an ideal, a place where you feel secure and

protected. I want you to think of it as the room where you do your writing. When you have spent about ten minutes in quiet revery, describe the beloved room.

The place you've just written about helps you to feel at ease, to feel nourished, warm, loved. It helps you to feel like a whole person: integrated, centred, in some important way *satisfied*. Remember that, even if no such room exists for you, you have written as though it does. What you have started to do is to create this place of support and satisfaction in yourself: you've begun to *make room* in your mind for your writer-self.

Now read your writing through. How do you feel when you read it? Emily Dickenson defined writing that *works* as 'something that makes me feel as though the top of my head is coming off'. She said she knew of no other way to assess the value of a piece. You can measure your own writing in this way, too. Ask yourself these questions:

Have I written all I wanted to write about the room, or have I left out something important? How do I feel when I read it – elated, stretched, sad, longing . . .? Or do I simply feel the same?

If the writing doesn't have a tangible effect on you, the writer, it is unlikely to stir or arouse others.

Reworking and strengthening

Now it is time to focus in detail upon your description. Take two felt-tip pens, of different colours, and underline in one colour all the words that catch the meaning you intended, that evoke strongly the feelings you have about the room. With the other pen, underline the parts you are not satisfied with, the phrases that fall short of expressing your meaning. Remember that you are your own best critic and only you can finally decide what it is you wanted to say.

Make a list on a separate sheet of paper of the flabby, vague, unfocused parts, so you can look at them out of context. What is it about them that dissatisfies you? Have you used words that are too familiar, worn-out similes, too many abstract nouns? As I go through some of the possible problems, check back to see which of them apply to the slack parts of your own writing.

Abstract nouns

These are words like 'joy', 'truth', 'misery', 'reflection', 'beauty' and 'ingratitude': naming-words for states of mind, intellectual concepts and categories. They are not words for physical things, like objects or parts of the body, but for states or processes that we cannot physically see or feel. Consequently, these words mean quite different things to different people. In creative writing they often only half do the job you used them for: they say more or less what you mean, but not exactly. For example, to write that you feel joyful in the room is a kind of vague shorthand. It reminds *you* how you felt there but leaves the reader with unanswered questions. The reader would have a much fuller impression of your state of mind if you lovingly evoked, say, the feel of a rug under your feet, the texture of the curtains, the smell of a shawl. Bringing in these things would make the room real to the reader – and new to you, the writer, because you'd have recreated it, having laid each of your senses open to it. The writing then becomes tangible, concrete, unique, instead of vague and hard to grasp.

Adjectives

Adjectives describe nouns. They give us extra knowledge about the thing itself. Here are some examples:
    a fierce temper
    a moving story
    a bitter quarrel
    an old man
You will notice that all the adjectives in this list are, to put it bluntly, boring. We've heard them so many times that they've ceased to have any effect. Check your work for boring adjectives. When you find one, ask yourself 'Do I really need *this* word or would the noun work better on its own? Can I find a noun that would convey the sense more clearly?' You may find that you do need an adjective, but not that one. When searching for the right adjective, bear in mind that your effect on the reader will be stronger if you can create physical sensation, if you can make the reader conjure up a colour, a

texture, a smell or a sound, rather than using a word like 'soothing', or 'lovely' or (worst of all) 'evocative'. Say, for example, there is a smell in the room that reminds you of your childhood. Don't be tempted to describe it as 'reminiscent' or 'reassuring'. Say exactly what the smell is. Is it mothballs or furniture polish or tobacco or vapour rub? If you 'give' the smell to the reader rather than using your own private shorthand, then the reader's own nose will do the work. The reader will smell the smell with you, with real participation and pleasure, rather than having to resentfully take your word for it. Also, you may find that in taking this concrete approach, you are making your nouns work harder for you and using fewer adjectives. This, again, will make your writing firmer, more substantial.

Adverbs

Adverbs describe verbs in the same way that adjectives describe nouns. They usually end in '–ly'. For example:

I walked slowly into the room.
Lovingly I touched the curtains.
I held the vase carefully.

Adverbs and adjectives contain similar problems: they both prevent the verb or the noun doing all the work it is capable of and rob a phrase of its necessary precision. Adverbs often do not render exactly *how* an action took place. Compare these sentences with the examples above:

I edged into the room.
I sidled into the room.   Which was it?

I fondled the curtains.
I caressed the curtains.   Which was it?

I lifted the vase between
    my thumb and forefinger.   Which was it?
I grasped the vase with both hands.

Different verbs offer alternative meanings in each of these sentences. They are all more exact than the sentences that rely on adverbs.

On the other hand, when adjectives and adverbs appear in clusters, they can produce a necessary *ritardando*. They force the reader to slow down, to dwell or brood on what is happening. They stop the eye from moving so fast, as in these sentences:

> Silently I circled the desk, pacing, prowling. Wooden, solid, it seemed to catch my eye, with its open, cleared space, its black, inviting pen.

You can see the way the underlined words, the adverb and adjectives, work to hold the reader still, locking their gaze upon the desk, which then seems to hypnotise both writer and reader.

Conversing with the spirits of place

There is a kind of mystical, powerful writing which does not simply evoke the spirit of place in order to determine action but seeks to converse with it, enter into a dialogue with all that has gone before. There is a kind of writing which lets the spirits of place speak. This writing may at first seem strange because it aims beyond the physical reality of our senses – addressing the past, the future and the spirits of those who are before and after. I want to write about it here so that new writers will know it exists and perhaps be brave enough to address this difficult aspect of our experience in their work.

In *The Colour Purple*, Alice Walker, through the letters of Nettie, a young black woman who has accompanied two missionaries to the home of the Olinka tribe in Africa, writes of the healing, life-giving qualities of the roofleaf plant, which embodies the spirit of place for the tribe:

> The people prayed to their gods and waited impatiently for the seasons to change. As soon as the rain stopped they rushed to the old roofleaf beds and tried to find the old roots. But of the endless numbers that had always grown there,

only a few dozen remained. It was five years before the
roofleaf became plentiful again. During those five years
many more in the village died. Many left, never to return.
Many were eaten by animals. Many, many were sick. The
chief was given all his storebought utensils and forced to walk
away from the village forever. His wives were given to other
men.

On the day when all the huts had roofs again from the
roofleaf, the villagers celebrated by singing and dancing and
telling the story of the roofleaf. The roofleaf became the thing
they worship.

Looking over the heads of the children at the end of this
tale, I saw slowly coming towards us, a large brown spiky
thing as big as a room, with a dozen legs walking slowly and
carefully under it. When it reached our canopy, it was
presented to us. It was our roof.

As it approached, the people bowed down.

The white missionary before you would not let us have this
ceremony, said Joseph. But the Olinka like it very much. We
know a roofleaf is not Jesus Christ, but in its humble way, is it
not God?

So there we sat, Celie, face to face with the Olinka God.
And Celie, I was so tired and sleepy and full of chicken and
groundnut stew, my ears ringing with song, that all that
Joseph said made perfect sense to me.

In *i is a long memoried woman*, Grace Nichols builds a stunning
sequence of poems out of just such a search for an imaginative
resting-place. Her memory ploughs back, past the beginning of
her own life, to Africa and slavery, to Guyana, sugar,
punishment on the plantation, loyalty and betrayal. Through
the story runs the gold thread of religion and magic:

alligator teeth
and feathers
old root and powder

I kyan not work this craft
this magic black
on my own strength

'Omen'

a thread which visibly supports the poet's intercessions with the spirits of her past. Through the search over three continents, homelessness and pain-memory, she is able to find a new tongue as the last poem, in a sort of quiet, cautious exultation, shows. I want to stress this connection between searching for home and finding a tongue, a writing voice, because I believe it to be fundamental to your own writing development.

A new angle of vision

In the exercise you are now about to attempt you will begin to see a familiar place through unfamiliar eyes. Your aim in this writing is to penetrate and supervene the way you normally see and construe your surroundings, to discover a new angle of vision. You may be unsympathetic to the transcendental or spiritual interpretations of reality in the writings I have just cited: that doesn't matter. I have written about them to show that spiritual journeys and beliefs are legitimate, fruitful ways of exploring the world and to encourage writers to go ahead with this kind of exploration if they so wish. If you do not wish to do so, then there are many other new angles of vision available to you: a child's viewpoint, for example, an animal's or the viewpoint of a stranger who may interpret familiar customs in unfamiliar ways. The painter Jean-Baptiste Chardin shatters our 'knowledge' of the world by presenting it to us in a new way, as if we were children and his bowl of fruit stood just above our eye-level. This 'newness', which is not really new but more an expansion of the rigid barriers of the individual self so that we see something as if we were not ourselves, is, I believe, one of the attributes of authentic, pleasurable art.

This exercise can be approached in two ways. Either

Take a familiar place and describe it through unfamiliar eyes.

or

Write about a journey to an unfamiliar place, a place that, when you visited it, fractured, ruptured or enlarged your understanding of the world.

Before you begin to write, think over what you have learned from the previous exercise. Think about clichés, abstract nouns, adjectives and adverbs. As you are trying to find a new angle of vision, it is particularly important that you avoid familiar or worn-out ways of writing. Though I am reluctant to lay down rules, I do find the following guidelines, set out in the Fowlers' *The King's English*, helpful as a sort of mental checklist for my own work:

1 Prefer the familiar word to the far-fetched.
2 Prefer the concrete word to the abstract.
3 Prefer the single word to the circumlocution.
4 Prefer the Saxon word to the Romance.
5 Prefer the short word to the long.

It is not necessary to stick rigidly to these. But if you do use a far-fetched or archaic word like *valetudinarian*, for example, as Jane Austen did on the first page of *Emma*, be sure you know why you are using it. Be sure, first, that no other word will do.

If you look closely at the Fowlers' five 'prefers', you will find that they are trying to guide you away from fancy writing. It is difficult to accept such guidance because often, in school, we are misled into thinking that fancy writing is good writing. We learn, mistakenly, that good writing is obscure, dense and full of hard words. We come to believe that good writing shows how clever we are. But when we read a page of powerful writing, we see immediately that it is not clever and has nothing to do with fanciness or obscurity. It uses plain words to their fullest effect so that we are stunned by how much the writer has enabled them to mean. When Maxim Gorki as a young man read a story by Guy de Maupassant, he marvelled 'why the plain, familiar words put together by a man into a story about the uninteresting life of a servant moved me so'.

Look at this section from Adrienne Rich's poem 'In the Wake of Home'.

But you will be drawn to places
where generations lie
side by side with each other:
fathers, mothers and children

in the family prayerbook
or the country burying-ground
You will hack your way through the bush
to the Jodensavanne
where the gravestones are black with mould
You will stare at old family albums
with their smiles   their resemblances
You will want to believe that nobody
wandered off became strange
no woman dropped her baby and ran
no father took off for the hills
no axe splintered the door
– that once at least it was in order
and nobody came to grief

Note how simply Adrienne Rich says what she has to say.
There is no superflux, no trailing extras: only a piercing
representation of the constant search for the secure, good-
enough home, the search that we persist in despite endless
disappointment and frustration.

Note the startling sparcity of adjectives: she uses them only
when she is forced to, so they seem pressed out of the nouns
through sheer weight of need. Look at these adjectives: *family*,
country, *black*, *old*, *strange*. They are tough, tensile; part of the
structure of the poem rather than decorative vines creeping
around it. Note particularly the total absence of adverbs. The
verbs do their own work. They don't need to lean on an adverb
for greater clarity.

Bring all you have learned to bear on the exercise. Find a
place to write, a room, and make room for your writer-self in
your mind.

3

Bringing your Descriptions to Life

CLOSE your eyes and sit quietly.
Bring into your inner field of vision – a lemon.
Examine it closely.
It is porous, with a little green dot in the middle of each pore.
Feel the knobbly, cool surface.
Imagine a knife.
You are slicing the lemon in half.
You raise one half to your mouth and sink your teeth into it.
What has happened?

This is an experiment suggested by José Silva and Philip Miele.
I'll wager that your salivary glands started pumping out liquid
as you imagined yourself biting into the lemon. The lemon
became real for you; your imagination tricked your body into
believing it would have to cope with a mouthful of pure citrus.
That is one of the things that writing does: it entices the reader
into an 'unreal' world, a world 'really' only composed of funny
marks on a page, and through those marks makes the reader
consider something which may form no part of normal life. It
throws words like *real* and *normal* into question, continually
challenges and subverts the things we take for granted, the
things we think we know.

As you work on the exercises in this chapter, I want you to
hold the lemon up steadily, as a guiding polestar. It engendered
a physical response. Make that a central aim in your
descriptive writing.

Here is a passage by Colette. As you read it, be aware of how it
makes you feel.

The caterpillar was perhaps asleep, moulded to the form of a supporting twig of box thorn. The ravages about her testified to her vitality. There were nothing but shreds of leaves, gnawed stems, and barren shoots. Plump, as thick as my thumb and over four inches long, she swelled the fat rolls of her cabbage-green body, adorned at intervals with hairy warts of turquoise blue. I detached her gently from her twig and she writhed in anger, exposing her paler stomach and all her spiky little paws that clung leechlike to the branch to which I returned her.

'But, mother, she has devoured everything!'

The grey eyes behind the spectacles wavered perplexedly from the denuded twigs to the caterpillar and hence to my face: 'But what can I do about it? And after all, the box thorn she's eating, you know, is the one that strangles honeysuckle.'

'But in any case, what can I do about it? I can hardly kill the creature.'

The scene is before me as I write, the garden with its sun-warmed walls, the last of the black cherries hanging on the tree, the sky webbed with long pink clouds. I can feel again beneath my fingers the vigorous resentment of the caterpillar, the wet, leathery hydrangea leaves, and my mother's little work-worn hand.

I can evoke the wind at will and make it rustle the stiff papery blades of the bamboos and sing, through the comb-like leaves of the yew, as a worthy accompaniment to the voice that on that day and on all other days, even to the final silence, spoke words that had always the same meaning.

'That child must have proper care. Can't we save that woman? Have those people got enough to eat? I can hardly kill the creature.'

My Mother's House

Look at the adjectives that apply to the caterpillar: *plump, thick, fat, cabbage-green, hairy, turquoise blue, spiky, leechlike*. Colette works at marshalling our feelings of revulsion at this voracious creature who has almost killed the poor box thorn. It is 'as thick as my thumb' – too big, surely. It must be a monster. She is setting her reader up to want the caterpillar dead. But then we

witness a sudden turn. The child Colette starts speaking to her
mother, lamenting the destruction of the plants. It is the
dialogue with the mother that performs the crucial shift,
enabling the reader to see the caterpillar in a new way, through
the mother's loving intercession. It is her nurturing, sustaining
tolerance, extended, it seems, to all the creatures in the garden,
that gives the initially repulsive caterpillar permission to live,
permission to carry on denuding the box thorn.

Colette's universe is tactile, first and last. The little girl *holds*
the caterpillar, plies it carefully from the twig to which it had
moulded itself. The mother's eyes *waver* on her daughter's face,
seeming to caress it. The sun has *warmed* the walls of the garden,
the cherries *hang* on the tree. The writer *can feel again* the
caterpillar, the hydrangea leaves and 'my mother's little
work-worn hand'. Everything touches, everything depends on
everything else. So her verbs are determinant in the making of
her effects. But perhaps more important are the adjectives. I
have discouraged the use of adjectives in the last two chapters
but here you can see them used with superb skill. Colette
positively revels in them. She often appends two to a single
noun (*long pink clouds*; *wet, leathery hydrangea leaves*; *stiff papery
blades*) to flesh out, give further fullness to the feeling she wants
to call forth in the reader.

Another part of Colette's method of *making round*, making
substantial, is her habit of moving backwards and forwards,
towards and away from the object. In this piece she starts very
near, so near she makes us want to vomit at the sight of the
caterpillar, and then she slowly moves away, gaining emotional
balance as she gains physical distance. She is able to tell us
more because she refuses to stand still. And just as she will not
keep the caterpillar restricted to one plane of vision, so also she
avoids obsessively restricting herself to the object. She allows
her mind to wander, following the associations that the
caterpillar calls up, in a kind of trance, knowing they will lead
her to where she needs to go.

Robert Lowell talked about the importance of this risk-
taking, this following of the associative details, when he was
interviewed for *Paris Review*.

Almost the whole problem of writing poetry is to bring it
back to what you really feel, and that takes an awful lot of

manoeuvring. You may feel the doorknob more strongly than some big personal event, and the doorknob will open into something that you can use as your own. A lot of poetry seems to me very good in the tradition, but it doesn't move me very much because it doesn't have personal vibrance to it. I probably exaggerate the value of it, but it's precious to me. Some little image, some detail you've noticed – you're writing about a little country shop, just describing it, and your poem ends up with an existentialist account of your experience. But it's the shop that started it off. You didn't know why it meant a lot to you. Often images and often the sense of the beginning and the end of a poem are all you have – some journey to be gone through between those things – you know that, but you don't know the details.

You have to take the risk of describing the doorknob, or the little country shop, because they may be the only details that can take you in – into the strange and wonderful labyrinth that is your writer-self. They may be the clew to reveal to you what you didn't think you wanted to say.

In Chapter 2 we embarked on the task of building a house for the writer-self, a beloved abode where the writer in you can live. Now it is time to bring movement and activity into those secure, quiet recesses. Bring a part of your own body into the house and watch how it moves.

The hand

You could probably use any part of your body for this exercise, but I suggest you start with your hand, your writing hand. Look at it. Place it on the table in front of you. Hold it in the air. Survey it on both sides. Clench it into a fist, then open it out. Look at it close up, then at a distance. Smell it. Feel it.

Here are a few words, all associated with the hand:

Mount of Venus	callus	ring	knuckle
phalange	scar	vein	life-line

You will find many others as you search your mind and, later, your dictionary.

As you explore your hand, allow your mind to wander over the significance of all its markings. Is there a scar? Where did it come from? What are the nails like and the cuticles? Let your hand tell you about yourself. Follow the clues on the hand.

Now write a description of your hand, taking the risks, following the associations that may lead nowhere but are more likely to lead exactly where you need to go. Write for as long as you can. Then rest. Leave yourself time to regain energy before starting the second part of the exercise. Imagine several movements your hand habitually makes – like holding a saw, peeling potatoes, rubbing in cream or making a pot of tea. How does your hand move? What does the state and movement of the hand indicate about its owner? Again, you need to make the hand do the telling, rather than bring in any extra information from outside.

When you have completed the whole exercise, scrutinise it, paying particular attention to your adjectives. The exercise in Chapter 1 questioned the use of these seductive parts of speech, so you will be healthily suspicious of their allure. But you have also read the passage from Colette and felt the sensuous materiality of the physical world she evokes with her adjectives, so you know too how strong an effect they can produce. With these two seemingly contradictory attitudes in mind, underline all the adjectives you've used. Look at each one in turn. Does it add a new dimension to its noun or would the noun be better off without it? Does it make you *feel* the meaning of the noun more fully? Is it a necessary part of the structure of your sentence? In Colette's description we have the sentence: 'There were nothing but shreds of leaves, gnawed stems and barren shoots.' The adjectives here are *gnawed* and *barren* and they are both structurally crucial to the meaning of the sentence: the sentence needs them. To test whether or not you need an adjective, all you have to do is reduce your sentence to the form of a telegram. Take it down to the bone, to as few words as possible. Which of the following would be more accurate?

a) nothing. stems and shoots.

b) gnawed stems barren shoots.

c) shreds stems shoots.

In (a) the 'nothing' seems to contradict the 'stems and shoots' and in (c) the 'shreds stems shoots' simply does not make sense.

We have to agree that Colette could not have done without her adjectives. Try to keep this exercise in your mind as you test out the necessity of your own adjectives.

Movement in the English sentence

For the second part of the exercise, you explored the sense of your hand in motion. Did you find this hard, harder than your description of the hand when it was still? Many writers, at first, feel frustrated and dissatisfied with this aspect of their work, rather as an archer does when he is learning to hit a moving target. If this is true for you, it may be worth considering the movement that lies immanent in every English sentence.

The English language is structured around its verbs. In each sentence, the subject and object are hinged together by the connecting verb, the verb that shows just what the subject is doing to the object.

She brought the hammer down on the nail.

We have the subject – *she*, the object – the hammer, and the indirect object – the nail. The nail is an indirect object because it is related to the verb through the preposition – *on*. It is the verb *to bring down* that forges the link between the otherwise *still* nouns and pronoun in the sentence. Without the verb they would be doing nothing. With the verb, we know that *she* is bringing the hammer down, and that the nail is being hammered. The verb calls all the nouns into a relationship of movement. From the Middle Ages to the present our language has hinged the words that represent people, animals and things together through verbs, through doing words. A verb always makes a link and it always represents some kind of movement.

That's all very well, you may object, but how do I make my verbs strong? How do I elicit a sense of bold movement in my sentences? I think Melquíades, the Gipsy in Gabriel Garcia Marquez' *A Hundred Years of Solitude*, gives an answer when he says 'Things have a life of their own. . . . It's simply a matter of waking up their souls.' For you as writer, this entails looking so hard at the world you write about that you begin to feel the minute, imperceptible movements within it and learn to give them their most appropriate names. Notice, for example, in the sentences quoted above, how Marquez uses the verb 'waking up' before the object 'souls'. He does not say 'It's simply a matter of showing their souls' or 'bringing out their souls'. Those verbs, though roughly appropriate, evoke no tingle of recognition in the reader: they are flat, inert. In 'waking up their souls' Marquez cuts straight to the heart of our earliest desires: to rise from the dead and be reunited with the souls of our lost ones, our dead forebears. 'Waking up' associates with new life, a new day, rousing from sleep, a new beginning. It is therefore an immensely energetic, hopeful verb – and because our states of mind are influenced, without our conscious knowledge, by the language that surrounds us, this energy and hope is 'fed' to us through the verb.

If you have enough living movement in your writing, if your nouns support each sentence and your verbs fly like flung ropes, or like shaking cobwebs, between them, *then* you are in a position to decorate it with adjectives and adverbs – but not until. If you load up your sentence with trifles before you've built it properly, it will of course fall down. William Carlos Williams made a lovely poem from this advice about architectural structure. It begins:

> Rather notice, mon cher,
> that the moon is
> tilted above
> the point of the steeple
> than that its colour
> is shell-pink.

'To a Solitary Disciple'

It is the angle of the moon and its position in relation to the steeple, rather than its colour, that is important to the poet. 'Shell-pink' would give a prettiness to the poem but a prettiness that is inappropriate because at this moment the moon has no connection with shells and every connection with the lines of the steeple.

It is hard to know for sure why this is so, why this firmness of outline is so important for the reader. When poetry, the oldest form of writing (apart from household accounts) came into being, it was written to serve a purpose: Sappho's lyrics entertained the guests at wedding parties; the bravery of warriors was celebrated in song to encourage the others and thrill the attendant crowds. Our word *verse* comes from the Latin *vers*, which means *furrow*. A verse covers a span of time, as does the ploughing of a furrow. People sang songs (lyric poetry simply meant songs accompanied by the lyre) while ploughing, scything, threshing and grinding corn. The song was a part of the day, a way of getting through the day tunefully, in rhythm. Perhaps the origins of song help to exlain why we still require a firm outline. Decorative details add further delight only if the outline has achieved its sure balance.

I think we still want our songs (poetry, story, play) to enable us to get through the day tunefully, to afford some new angle of vision that will 'give' us the world in a new way, elicit our love for the world again, though our faculties may be tired, though the world may be desolated. And the writer can only conjure up this gift for the reader if he/she is prepared, first of all, to write plainly what he/she believes to be true, rather than fall for the surface sweetmeats which seem to satisfy but which, like sugar, leave the reader hungry minutes later. Hemingway said, rightly I think, 'The most essential gift for a good writer is a built-in, shock-proof, shit detector. This is the writer's radar and all great writers have had it.' For 'shit' we can also read 'sugar' or 'soap' of the '–opera' variety. Some readers have grown accustomed to reading/watching/eating shit because they have never been offered anything else. This is an unspeakable tragedy. As a writer, your sovereign responsibility is to produce real food by making truthful representations. The first poets played their part in the making of bread: today's writers grow a different kind of food but still provide a nourishment neither they nor their readers can do without.

Cutting it down to the bone

During the 14th century, Japanese poets began to develop the form of verse we now call the *haiku*. Haiku or *hokku* literally means 'starting verse' because it was originally the beginning of an older verse form called the *tanka*. They are the sparest verses imaginable, so short that there is no room for anything but the concentrated feeling. Because of their brevity, Japanese students of poetry and religion are given the task of reading and writing *haiku*. One of the aims of the *haiku* writer is to avoid 'putting words between the truth and ourselves', to write the 'transparent' poetry that T. S. Eliot strove for, poetry that tries to close the distance between the word and the object it represents.

Words are not things: we have to accept that. There is a perilous gap between the table I write on and the word 'table'. The writer works at the impossible task of creating a poem, a narrative, which tries to narrow the gap between the signal and what is signalled: tries to reverse the separation between the world and what we write about the world. This effort to unite what cannot be united lies at the heart of the *haiku* and accounts for some of its tense, sad loveliness.

Here are some of the verses of Matsuo Bashō, an early master of the form:

The beginning of all art:
a song when planting a rice field
in the country's inmost part.

On a journey, ill,
and over fields all withered, dreams
go wandering still

'Leaving the house of a friend'
out comes the bee
from deep among peony pistils –
oh, so reluctantly!

As you can see, though each of these poems 'simply' describes a moment that has something to do with the natural world, other thoughts and messages come through at the same time. The *haiku* poets aimed to condense many meanings into each phrase, so that the poem should speak of something that has both a particular and a general significance.

It is this degree of concentration I want you to work towards, using the *haiku* both as a point of departure and as a discipline you frequently return to. These are the formal dimensions of the *haiku*: five syllables in the first line; seven in the second; five in the third. The form can be made more flexible in English, (the translator of Bashō has bent the rules considerably) because it does not possess the same internal formal necessity as it would in Japanese, but try to stick roughly to the proposed number of syllables. Your own *haiku* can have 'movement' as its subject, 'my town', 'Spring' or whatever has moved you to powerful feeling. It can be funny or sad. You can experiment with the creation of different tones and moods in your three allotted lines.

Below are a few *haiku* written by students in a writing class. I include them here to encourage you to write about anything at all. Among the qualities for which Bashō's *haiku* are revered are 'a desire to use every instant to the uttermost; an appreciation of this even in natural objects; a feeling that nothing is alone, nothing unimportant; a wide sympathy; and an acute awareness of relationships of all kinds, including that of one sense to another.' Notice the verbs in the *haiku* below and the way they catch the emotion of a single moment.

'Thirteen floors up'
if you fall
off the balcony
you've had it
Smaaack!

Nigel Young

I need to kiss you.
You must be joking, she said,
Out here, in the street?

Blowing top notes
She lifts her trombone up high
I watch her breathless.

He is everywhere
This younger greedy brother
Wanting to join in.

Mel Kathchild

4
Making your Characters Speak

WRITERS often come to the problem of dialogue in fear and trembling. 'How do I make people speak naturally?' 'What would they say here?' 'What would he keep to himself there?' In our everyday lives we learn about people in many ways: the way they eat, their clothes, their scent, their movements, the way they hold themselves. But speech is one of the most revealing aspects of a person. We listen to the tone of their voice. Does it rankle and jar or do we feel at home with the sound? In Britain we often listen for a person's accent. It tells us where they come from. Often it tells us about their background or which social group they identify with. A dialect, too, where syntax and grammar work differently to 'standard' English, the sort taught in our educational institutions, shows that someone has consciously or unconsciously chosen not to abandon the speech patterns of their region for the blander cadences of BBC English.

We tend to assess people through what they say and the way they say it, to come to conclusions about whether we will like someone from the way they present themselves in words. D. H. Lawrence does it in a poem called 'The Oxford Voice'.

When you hear it languishing
and hooing and cooing and sidling through the
                              front teeth,
          the Oxford voice
          or worse still
          the would-be Oxford voice
you don't even laugh any more, you can't.

MAKING YOUR CHARACTERS SPEAK

Here is Lawrence's anger, disciplined into a poem, about an accent and a quality of voice that speaks its own privilege and superiority. To write this poem, Lawrence evidently had to listen very hard to the Oxford voice. He knows what happens inside the mouth and how the sounds are emitted. He *gives* us the voice, so we can examine it ourselves and ask our own questions about it, even though he does not cite directly anything the Oxford voice says. I think that Lawrence gives us our first clue in the writing of dialogue: that we must listen and, having listened, ask ourselves how we feel about the voice we've just heard.

We need to know how we feel about the sounds because if a certain accent or tone is anathema to us we often instinctively turn away from it, forget it. We make it impossible to use, when in fact that voice might greatly strengthen our writing. Also, if we turn away uncritically from a voice we hate or fear, then we are turning away from a source of conflict – and conflict is one of the writer's richest foods. If you can hold your feelings and examine them, force yourself to hear the voice and ask why it produces the response that it does, you are beginning to get the better of it, to break the fearful silence that surrounds it and, incidentally, to add another voice to your writing repertoire. Take this case, for example. One afternoon while I was in the USA, I received four obscene telephone calls. I was alone in the house and extremely frightened. When I called the police, they instructed me to write down everything the caller had said. I didn't want to. I just wanted to forget it had ever happened. But I forced myself to write it all down and, as I wrote it, it began to lose its power over me. I was containing the threats in written words: I was taking control. I kept the piece of paper and, after I returned home and thought more about the episode, I transformed it into a poem. It was important to me not to be silenced by the fear the anonymous caller invoked. After I'd finished the poem I felt triumphant that I'd broken my fear-silence. I also thought I'd written a better poem because I'd struggled with the voice, forced myself to hear it again in my mind and to reply to it. This dialogue went into the poem.

The voice of the place

If you come from a certain town or region, you will know what
the different voices mean better than someone who comes from
outside because you've learned the code. Some South
American students, for whom English was a second or third
language, found it impossible to read and understand
Lawrence's play *The Daughter-in-Law*, a play where the use of
Eastwood dialect renders it only easily accessible to those at
home with varieties of regional English. *You* have to decide how
much dialect will go into your writing and to do this you must
be sure of your subject and of how wide you want your audience
to be. Lawrence could express the strongest emotion through
dialogue that used dialect – as in this section from *John Thomas
and Lady Jane*.

> He looked at her still with a touch of resistance.
> 'I don't *care!*' she said. 'I'll give you all the money
> tomorrow, and let you buy what you like, if you'll take it.'
> 'No no!' he said, sinking into sullen silence. Then he
> looked up suddenly, beginning in a harsh voice, then
> breaking suddenly into broad dialect: 'I love – Ah luv thee!
> Ah luv thee!' He took her hand and pressed it against his
> belly. 'But tha wunna want ter ma'e me feel sma', shall ter?
> Let me be mysen, and let me feel as if tha' wor littler than me!
> dunna ma'e me feel sma', an' *down!* – else I canna stop wi' thee.
> Let me luv thee my own road, as if I was bringin' the money
> 'ome. I canna help it. Tha can laugh at me – but dunna want
> ter ma'e me feel sma'! Laugh at me – I like thee ter laugh at
> me! But be nice to me, an' dunna be big! For I feel I've got no
> place in the world, an' no mortal worth to nobody, if not to
> thee. An' I dunna want ter hate everthing. It ma'es me feel as
> if I'd swallowed poison, an' had a bellyful, in a way.

Notice that Parkin is able to say what he truly means only after
he has broken into dialect. It is as though Lawrence was
acknowledging that it is hard for human beings to say what
they feel and that we often have to search for the form of words
before we can find the words themselves. Just as we, in our
writing, have to find the words that fit what we are trying to

express, the most appropriate words, so the characters in a story, novel or poem also have to discover the language that is fitting. Again, to learn to render this we have to listen to how people speak. How does a particular person begin? Does she dive straight to the point or does she circle around, feeling for what she wants to say? Does another person begin with 'Well, you know . . . .' or any other characteristic expression? In *John Thomas and Lady Jane*, Connie is distinguished from Parkin by the type of English she uses (middle-class, standard). We can always tell who is speaking because they speak different languages.

If we listen acutely, we hear that everyone speaks a language that is in some way unique. Each person uses words in his or her own way; avoids some words, uses others frequently. We know this because sometimes we may use a word which we ourselves consider innocuous, only to find that it produces a strong emotional response in someone else. It carries a different meaning for them. Listening to the speech of those around us, we begin to discern how character reveals itself through words and also how people use words to veil themselves.

Conventions for writing dialogue

You may know what you want to write but remain unsure about the 'rules' for getting your dialogue onto the page. Let us look at three different ways of showing speech. We need to be aware that 'rules' (which are really just agreed-on conventions) are changing all the time, particularly since the line between inner voices and outer voices has become blurred.

Here is a passage from Kay Boyle's *Plagued by the Nightingale*.

"Come back, come back!" she shouted, but he pretended that he had not heard her at all.

Down through the sea she splashed to him. If she held his hand, she thought, surely he could run faster with her than quite alone. Surely no tide could have them if they clasped hands and fled from it side by side.

"Nicolas, Nicolas, Nicolas," she cried to him.

"Eh?" he said, lifting his head to her as if in irritation. "What is it you want?"

"Come back, come back," she shouted, "the tide is coming in!"

"Well, what about it?" said Nicolas. She was coming close to him now.

"Give me your hand, Nicol," she said. You must come back."

"Why should I come back?" said Nicolas. He stood looking at her in his dark, gloomy way. "What reason is there for me to go back?"

She had grabbed his hand and his cane firmly in her hands and was trying to pull him back through the water.

This is the traditional and still most widely-used way of making your characters speak. Everything Nicolas or Bridget says is wrapped in inverted commas, which open as the character opens his mouth and close as he closes it. Each speech is followed by 'she cried to him' or 'said Nicolas' to make it absolutely clear who's saying what.

You don't always need every 'he said' and 'said she'. They can be tedious if repeated too often – and if each character does have her own recognisable pattern of language, then the reader will know who is speaking without being told. If you removed all the he saids and she saids from the writing above you would still know who was saying what because Nicolas and Bridget are doing different things. Their actions distinguish them from one another. Bridget also calls Nicolas by his name more than once, which 'marks' him for the reader.

In a story from Cynthia Ozick's *Levitation*, the dialogue is made to move faster by leaving out the explanatory tail-pieces. Here is an argument between Mayor Puttermesser and Xanthippe, the golem with whose help the Mayor has gained political power.

The Mayor upbraids Xanthippe: "It's enough. I don't want him around here. Get rid of him."

Xanthippe writes: "Jealousy!"

"I'm tired of hearing complaints from the cook. This is Gracie Mansion, it's not another kind of house."

"Jealousy! He used to be yours."
"You're stirring up scandal."
"He brings me presents."
"If you keep this up, you'll spoil everything."
"My mother has purified the City."
"Then don't foul it."
"I am in contemplation of my future."

Each character still begins a new line, so we know when a new person is speaking, but the 'said Puttermessers' and 'said Xanthippes' are pared to the bone: we have to deduce who is speaking from what they say and the way they say it. This affects the pace of the dialogue. It gives an impression of urgency, even breathlessness. We can tell that the writer is eager to take us to the climax. Dialogue of this type can be used effectively when the reader has settled into a story, knows exactly who's who by the way they speak, and is as anxious as the author to reach the crisis point. If it is used too early, it can be confusing so that the reader has to 'count back' to find out who is speaking and readers are not generally prepared to do that too often.

It is not crucial to start a new line each time a new person speaks, as long as the writer makes us *know* the speaker. John Betjeman bumps the speakers into one another in *Summoned By Bells*.

"I *love* Miss Usher," Audrey said. "Don't you?"
"Oh yes," I answered. "So do I" said Joc.
"We vote Miss Usher topping. Itchicoo!"
What was it I had done? Made too much noise?
Increased Miss Tunstall's headache? Disobeyed?
After Miss Usher had gone home to Frant,
Miss Tunstall took me quietly to the hedge:
"Now shall I tell you what Miss Usher said
About you, John?" "Oh please, Miss Tunstall, do!"
"She said you were a common little boy."

Three people talking are harder to handle than two, so Betjeman uses names more than Ozick. But Audrey, John and Joc are not facing one another in confrontation, as Puttermesser and Xanthippe are. They are three friends who have put their heads together to discuss the merits of a teacher, so they don't need the splendid isolation of a separate line each. Each speaker springs off from the one before rather than opposes him. The form by which the dialogue is represented is the one that best fits the mood and subject of the dialogue. Notice, though, that when a particularly telling statement is being made ("We vote Miss Usher topping. Itchicoo!" and "She said you were a common little boy.") it *does* have a line to itself. This is a way of drawing our attention and slowing us down so we concentrate more closely.

Inverted commas can even be abandoned in some cases. Look at this passage from James Joyce's *A Portrait of the Artist as a Young Man.*

– Do you remember, he said, when we knew each other first? The first morning we met you asked me to show you the way to the matriculation class, putting a very strong stress on the first syllable. You remember? Then you used to address the jesuits as father, you remember? I ask myself about you: *Is he as innocent as his speech?*
– I'm a simple person, said Davin. You know that. When you told me that night in Harcourt Street those things about your private life, honest to God, Stevie, I was not able to eat my dinner. I was quite bad. I was awake a long time that night. Why do you tell me those things?
– Thanks, said Stephen. You mean I am a monster.
– No, said Davin, but I wish you had not told me. A tide began to surge beneath the calm surface of Stephen's friendliness.
– This race and this country and this life produced me, he said. I shall express myself as I am.

What does it mean to get rid of speech marks altogether? I think what is most evident is that the boundary line between what is spoken aloud and what is spoken inwardly, to oneself, becomes blurred. What Stephen says and what Stephen thinks begin to merge because the punctuation mark that indicates 'now my character speaks' is missing. Joyce does use the dash, however, to show that he is moving from descriptive narrative to direct expression. Does the dash have a different feel about it, different to the feel of speech marks? I think it does. To me it emphasises the speech more strongly, shows the characters *breaking into* speech rather than hanging up their speech marks to say 'Please, may I speak now?' Notice that Joyce doesn't even use speech marks for a speech within a speech, as where Stephen says – . . . I ask myself about you: *Is he as innocent as his speech?* The words are italicised instead, which makes them stand out, as if starred by the new typeface.

We have now looked at four different ways of showing dialogue on the page and seen how each way is appropriate to the dialogue it represents. You may encounter other ways of showing speech, ways you can use in your own writing. You choose the form that best suits what you need to say, remembering always that the forms exist to help you say what you want to. They're not sacrosanct or eternal – even though, once you've chosen a form, it achieves its own custom of permanence. Once you start on a convention, you stay with it until the end of your story or poem.

What we say and what we write

To explore the differences between written dialogue and what people actually say to one another we need to examine the relationship between the written word and other aspects of lived experience. In order to test out the connections between the two, try transcribing a conversation you've overheard on a bus, in a dentist's waiting-room or round a meal table. You won't be able to catch all of it but get as much down as you can. It doesn't matter what the conversation is about: however inconsequential it seems, treat it as though all of it is important. Work at your transcription for four or five minutes. It's probably full of abbreviations and emendations because you've had to rush to get it all down, so take it home and write it up into recognisable dialogue.

Now look at it. What do you think of it? Does it interest you? Is it going anywhere? Do the characters reveal themselves through what they say? Your answers to these questions will begin to tell you how close you want your dialogue to come to the conversation you heard. If you thought what the people said possessed an intrinsic interest, if you wrote it down verbatim and pictured yourself as a sort of secretary to the outside world, recording something which had its own imaginative value but would otherwise have been lost, then you are one sort of writer – a naturalist. If, on the other hand, you judged the conversation you heard to be trivial and inconsequential and found yourself only selecting certain parts of it: if you changed it, rewrote it, rethought it completely so that it accorded with your own notion of how that conversation *should* have proceeded, then you are another sort of writer. You could be a realist, an expressionist or a *nouveau romancier* but the point is that you are not content to record things as they are. You believe that artistic expression involves some kind of radical transformation.

I myself think that the writer's relation to things as they are changes according to what he or she is writing. Sometimes we come very close to the world outside, for example when we hear someone say the words we need for a piece of writing we're involved in we commit it lovingly to memory so we can use it. On the other hand, we sometimes withdraw completely from words as they are spoken, for example when we work on a dialogue that breaks certain social taboos, that shows characters saying things we cannot imagine people actually daring to say.

I want to recount an experience that has stayed with me ever since it happened, something that transformed an uneventful journey home from work. I think it illustrates the difference separating the writer's dialogue from the dialogue of everyday life.

One evening, tired, hungry and frazzled, I caught the tube home from Central London. Anyone who has done this will know the feeling of being cramped in with other tired people, strap-hanging, sweating after a day at work. Conversation is almost non-existent. People don't have the energy to say much, preferring to use their newspapers to keep others at bay. From out of this irritated lassitude, a conversation began to reach me. When I looked up I saw it was coming from two smartly dressed men on the long bench-seat opposite. It went like this:

'Where are you off to over the weekend?'
'Oh, I thought we'd drive down to Stephanie's. She's just

bought a little place down in Sussex. You know, fresh air, good food, wine, reading the Sunday newspapers out of reach of the telephone. . . .'
He went on at some length, with a slightly exaggerated middle-class accent, to enthuse over the pleasures of privileged country living. The man next to him smiled in total agreement. Then suddenly, the man on his other side, who was dressed as a hippy and had very long hair, said 'How boring!' The first man stopped in mid-flow and turned. 'I beg your pardon?' 'I said "How boring".' 'That's very impertinent of you. How do you know it's boring? I might think the things you do are boring. That book you're reading, for example, what is it?' 'Graham Greene's *The Quiet American.*' 'Well, I know for a fact that Graham Greene is a very boring writer and that *The Quiet American* is his most boring book.'

By this time the whole tube carriage was riveted to the three men. It was delightful – not only to hear two of them boast so loudly about the lotus-eating weekend but to see what they said so effectively and hilariously challenged by a person from a different social group. I felt elated, and I think the other passengers did too, that the taboo against expressing oneself on the tube had been temporarily broken. The three men got off together, still avidly discussing Graham Greene. Everyone shifted around in the seats and relaxed. They all looked somehow looser. I certainly felt it had done me good and now whenever I recall it, I smile.

Afterwards I learned that the three men were actors, part of a company called *The Theatre of the Tube.* And when I thought back over the conversation, I realised that it was an extremely unlikely thing to have happened. Men don't usually conduct loud, enthusiastic duologues about rural delights (not English men, anyway) and it was even more unusual to hear someone butt in with 'Excuse me, I couldn't help overhearing, and what you're saying is absolute rubbish.' It was what I'd always wanted to happen but thought never would. When I say it like that I'm struck by how near that is to Pope's 'What e'er was thought / But ne'er so well expressed' definition of poetry. It seems to me that art of all kinds emerges out of deep human needs, needs that cannot be met anywhere else. That conversation would never have happened spontaneously. The three men might have thought those things but not have said them aloud. So the actors were speaking what would otherwise have remained unspoken.

Now look back at the extracts from Lawrence, Boyle, Ozick, Betjeman and Joyce. How much of that dialogue can you imagine actually being said? Can you imagine a shy working-class man (as Parkin is in *John Thomas and Lady Jane*) *comin' out wi'* that lengthy, passionate declaration of love for Connie? I can't. I can imagine him saying "Ah luv thee, but dunna ma'e me feel sma' " but it's hard for me to picture the careful explanation and vindication of himself that comes after. I think he *could* have said it but that he wouldn't have. That is to say, he could think through those ideas and feelings and in theory he could say them aloud but his shyness and his social position and the conventions about men expressing their feelings would have prevented him. That's if Parkin were a man in real life. But he's not, he's a character in a novel. In the novel I can believe he is saying such things, perhaps because I am hearing his voice in my head, in the privacy of my own mind (I am *thinking* him) and I am extremely relieved to hear him say them because his words bring to an end a certain kind of conflict between himself and Connie. The only way the conflict can ease is if Connie and Parkin communicate with one another. They may communicate more fully than they would in real life but this is to my advantage as the reader because it increases my relief and my pleasure. It allows me to savour the end of the conflict, to enjoy it in a way I could not have done if it had really happened, that is if a few words had been exchanged, spoken with difficulty through the barbed-wire taboos that separate people in so-called intimate relationships. In the novel, Parkin's declaration leaves us in no doubt about what he feels and what he wants. Lawrence has given us something we could not easily get otherwise: he has given us *thought* spoken as *language*.

Look through the other extracts too. How much of the dialogue can you imagine being spoken in those circumstances? Nicolas and Bridget in *Plagued by the Nightingale* I can understand. It's the sort of "You stupid boy, stop trying to

MAKING YOUR CHARACTERS SPEAK 49

drown yourself" speech I can imagine I would deliver if I were
dragging a recalcitrant lad back to land. The Ozick extract is a
particular case because it is a fantasy but it is the kind of clipped
talk I think likely between two opponents who are squaring up
to fight one another. The *Portrait of the Artist* extract is more
difficult, in the same way I think the Lawrence extract is
difficult. I can see Stephen and Davin thinking these things
about one another but find it hard to imagine them expressing
them aloud – if they existed as real people. But again, they
don't, and Joyce is enabling us to hear something we could not
hear outside his novel. The dialogues of both Joyce and
Lawrence are performing what Eliot would call 'raids on the
inarticulate'. They expand for us what we are able to think and
say.

When Virginia Woolf first read Lawrence, she said she felt as
if a curtain had been thrown back, so she could see, clearly, for
the first time, the intensity of family relationships. That is what
I take to be the goal of all writing: to open up fenced-off plots, to
water tracts of land that have dried out, to make accessible
thoughts and feelings that readers never knew they had or
thought they were not allowed to have. In this sense writing,
and particularly the writing of dialogue, performs a
provocative, subversive and liberating role. It opens wider the
realm of the possible.

Writing your own conflict

Rows between characters offer a superb opportunity for
dialogue writing. Look at this passage from Ian McEwan's
'Psychopolis':

> At roughly the same time Terence said, 'Another objection
> to Christianity is that it leads to passive acceptance of social
> inequalities because the real rewards are in . . . .'
> And Mary cut across George in protest. 'Christanity has
> provided an ideology for sexism now, and capitalism . . . .'
> 'Are you a communist?' George demanded angrily,
> although I was not sure who he was talking to. Terence was
> pressing on loudly with his own speech. I heard him mention
> the Crusades and the Inquisition.

'More evil perpetrated in the name of Christ than . . . this has nothing to do with . . . to the persecution of women herbalists as witches . . . Bullshit. It's irrelevant . . . corruption, graft, propping up tyrants, accumulating wealth at the altars . . . fertility goddess . . . bullshit . . . phallic worship . . . look at Galileo . . . this has nothing to . . . .' I heard little else because now I was shouting my own piece about Christianity. It was impossible to stay quiet.

Notice how they are all so excited that they can no longer listen to one another. Four monologues begin at once, with the pace of the argument and the gaps in understanding between the four participants shown by the pregnant, rushing rows of dots. Remember this when you write an argument: that they depend, to a large extent, on the antagonists not hearing one another – for if they heard and understood one another, then a measure of sympathy would be extended and the continuance of the row would be threatened. All you need is an 'I know what you mean' or 'I can see what you're getting at' for an entirely different kind of discussion to begin. To maintain the row's high pitch of energy, you need to make sure that sympathy is withheld by all parties. This often entails making each character in some way deaf to what the others are saying.

Now imagine yourself once again in the room you love. You feel protected and at rest and you have a great desire for solitude. There is a knock at the door. It opens, without waiting for your 'Come in'. Suddenly, there facing you, is the person you least want to see at that moment. You may not dislike the person (or alternatively, you may) but you don't want to see them *then*, at all. You make it quite clear that you need to be alone, but the other person either cannot or will not hear. Your control breaks. A row ensues.

Write the whole incident.

5

Making a Short Story

WHAT makes a short story? Characters, a setting, action of some kind, dialogue perhaps. These are the traditional ingredients but you will find stories that omit one or more of these to create a new effect or emphasis. You have worked on all these aspects of narrative in your exercises. If you mixed all your pieces of writing together, would they make a story? Or does a short story need something else, and if so what is it?

I think it does. That 'something' could be the letter in the back of the drawer that nobody finds until it is too late. It is the unheard-of, something that only the author knows: the vital knowledge that gives the author control over both the characters and the readers of the book. You may object that I'm only describing the kind of action that occurs in whodunnit stories – but look again at the short fictions that have moved you. Can you say where the appeal lies? What is it about them that speaks to you, that calls forth such a strong response that at the end you feel satisfied, nourished, as though something new had taken place? It is crucial that you answer these questions for yourself, because through learning to understand the source of your own reading pleasure you will begin to see how to produce that pleasure for other readers.

T. S. Eliot aptly describes what happens in many short stories in 'The Love Song of J. Alfred Prufrock';

> Let us go, through certain half-deserted streets,
> The muttering retreats
> Of restless nights in one-night cheap hotels
> And sawdust restaurants with oyster-shells:
> Streets that follow like a tedious argument
> Of insidious intent

To lead you to an overwhelming question . . .
Oh, do not ask, 'What is it?'
Let us go and make our visit.

A character will be led towards his own 'overwhelming question'. Some crisis, however small, will force a change in the fabric of his life and the author will understand and control this crisis, this change. Does the form of this story sound off echoes for you? Have you seen it before, in Maupassant's 'La Parure' ('The Necklace') or Henry James's 'The Beast in the Jungle'?

Take some time to *bathe* in short stories and look particularly at what the author is doing with the characters and the setting. In the two I've just mentioned you will find a character who lives many years without the benefit of some vital knowledge, something they really needed to know. Had they known it, their lives would have been completely different. The reader, too, labours on without this knowledge. It is revealed to the reader at the same time as the character. Too late. The character cannot benefit by what he or she now knows and all the reader can do is reflect on all that has been lost or missed. This is called *irony*.

Irony *n.*, *pl.* + **nies. 1.** the humorous or mildly sarcastic use of words to imply the opposite of what they normally mean. **2.** an instance of this, used to draw attention to some incongruity or irrationality. **3.** incongruity between what is expected to be and what actually is, or a situation or result showing such incongruity.

Collins English Dictionary

In 'La Parure' and 'The Beast in the Jungle' the knowledge which, if the characters had possessed it would have changed their whole lives, is revealed right at the end. We can only imagine what they do with it. And really, because the story ends there, it doesn't matter what the characters do with it: the point is, what does *the reader* do with it? For it seems to me, that in this type of story, the author is teaching the reader a terrible lesson, is saying 'Look! This is what happens when a person lives locked inside a view of the world that does not take the existence of others into account'.

Another word for 'delusion' is 'mistake', 'fault' or 'flaw'. Maupassant's 'La Parure' tells the story of a woman who is bitterly dissatisfied with her lower middle-class, unexciting husband. She dreams of being adored, the centre of attention. When she and her husband have the chance to attend a ball, a rather grand function, she borrows an exquisite necklace from an acquaintance. They go to the ball, she is indeed admired by everyone there but when they get home she realises she has lost the necklace. She spends the next ten years taking in washing, slaving away to pay back the money they borrowed to replace it. At the end of this time, worn-down and aged far beyond her years, she meets the woman who lent her the necklace. The acquaintance is shocked, asks what could have happened to bring about this change, so the main character explains. At the end of the story, the lender admits 'It was paste' to the woman who has laboured for ten years. The fault or flaw here seems to lie in the woman's original dissatisfaction. The story leads us to ask questions like 'Why was she so displeased by her own life?', 'If she disliked it so much, why didn't she change it, instead of just dreaming of being adored?', 'Why didn't she value what she had?', 'Why didn't she buy a necklace she *knew* was paste, for the ball?'

We are witness to a disaster, a word which means 'a fault in the stars' (dis-aster). But since Cassius's 'The fault lies not in our stars, but in ourselves' we have found it hard to take external circumstances as the sole cause of terrible events. And because we are reading the story, we are at an imaginative level participating in the events, recognising aspects of ourselves in the main character. We see our own dissatisfactions, our own pointless, unfocused longings in her and we are forced, because we are shown the terrible thing that happens to her, to question aspects of ourselves which might otherwise remain unexamined. Four lines of T. S. Eliot's 'East Coker' come to mind here:

The wounded surgeon plies the steel
That questions the distempered part.
Beneath the bleeding hands we feel
The sharp compassion of the healer's art

The writer writes out of his own wounds and in doing so he enables his reader to experience emotional change, emotional growth, healing without having to suffer the same fate as his character. In this type of short story, large claims are made about the effect of the reading experience. The underlying thrust is morality: the woman in 'La Parure' loses everything by her pointless longing. A delusion and a vain hope are opened up for us, so we can witness their terrible results. The author makes use of irony to point out a moral conclusion. We, the readers, are the only ones who can learn from the story: the characters have already lost everything.

Now try this out for yourself. Walk around the streets, looking carefully at people's faces. Wander aimlessly, taking your time. You will see a face that tells you something: there is a story in that face. Walk on and, during the course of half-an-hour's walk, imagine the secret the face reveals/conceals. Go home and write the story of the secret, divulging it to your reader at the very end. It is important that you *imagine* the secret, rather than steal it from a face you already know. When we write the stories of people we know, we often fall into the trap of identifying too strongly with our subject and not giving the reader enough to go on because the material is too familiar to us.

When I read out 'La Parure' to a writing class, I noticed that the penny dropped with some people just before the author disclosed the secret. Murmurs of 'It's paste' went around as I read the conversation between the two women. The reader *is* put into the position of detective in stories of this kind, so it's as well to remember that your story, too, will be combed for clues. Make sure that you tell your readers everything they need to know, so that when you deliver up your secret, they will greet it with absolute belief, with 'Of course. I should have guessed.'

Swallowing a glass of vodka

Not all short stories surprise the reader at the end. Some build up a sense of forboding that is either confirmed or denied, some make us laugh all the way through, some seem written only to outrage. It is hard to find a common thread. Perhaps we need to

look, not at their content or form, but at their effect when we try
to ascertain what is true for all of them – at least, all the stories
that *work*. Anton Chekhov said that reading a short story 'feels
rather like swallowing a glass of vodka'. Does that seem right to
you? A quick, sharp beverage that hits you in the throat and
then in the guts; that changes, perhaps only for a time, your
way of seeing the world? A novel would be different: a source of
sustenance over days or weeks, something to keep you going.
There may be surprises, but they are woven into the fabric, the
kind of surprises you live with. In the short story there doesn't
seem to be that kind of time – for the characters to digest and
integrate the surprise into their lives. They experience it and
they are gone. The task of integration is left to the reader.

So what *is* a story? A piece of writing where something
happens? Or where nothing happens? (Montaigne said that
'even constancy is a more sluggish form of movement'.) Where
something is seen to change? But how do we show change? By
showing things-as-they-are, then showing them penetrated by
the catalyst, the agent that embodies the will-to-change.

What is your earliest memory of a story where something or
somebody changed? Because our conscious memories are
selective, because we remember stories that meant something
to us, that *spoke* to us, your answer will reveal to you a great deal
about the way you used stories when you were a child.

Until recent years, when the popularity of the short story has
greatly increased, it was looked upon as a sort of poor relation
to the novel, something the novelist did to occupy idle time,
rather like wittling wood. But if we include children's literature
in our survey, then the short story occupies a more permanently
important place. Our first introduction to the world of the
imagination is made in fairy tales, folk tales, shaggy dog stories,
elaborately told jokes and the dramatic scenarios we invent for
ourselves, our friends and our toys.

Psychologists believe that we hold on to certain stories
because they enable us to make sense of an otherwise confusing
world – that we learn through stories and see our way through
to maturity with their help.

In early adolescence a girl had been fascinated by 'Hansel
and Gretel', and had derived great comfort from reading

and re-reading it, fantasizing about it. As a child, she had
been dominated by a slightly older brother. He had, in a way,
shown her the path, as Hansel did when he put down the
pebbles which guided his sister and himself back home. As
an adolescent, this girl continued to rely on her brother, and
this feature of the story felt reassuring. But at the same time
she also resented the brother's dominance. Without her
being conscious of it at the time, her struggle for
independence rotated around the figure of Hansel. The story
told her unconscious that to follow Hansel's lead led her
back, not forward, and it was also meaningful that although
Hansel was the leader at the story's beginning, it was Gretel
who in the end achieved freedom and independence for both,
because it was she who defeated the witch. As an adult, this
woman came to understand that the fairy tale had helped her
greatly in throwing off her dependence on her brother, as it
had convinced her that an early dependence on him need not
interfere with her later ascendancy. Thus, a story which for
one reason had been meaningful to her as a young child
provided guidance for her at adolescence for quite a different
reason.

Bruno Bettelheim, *The Uses of Enchantment.*

Think back to all the stories that affected you strongly as a
child. Can you remember which part exerted the special
emotional pull, the part that brought you back to the story
again and again? And what about the part the stories played in
your emotional development? If you love a story, you know it
all the way through. Did you, like the girl Bettelheim speaks of,
dwell on different stages at different times, according to your
need? When we include fairy stories in our consideration of 'the
short story', we realise how central they have been to our
childhood, adolescence and adulthood, too: how we have pored
eagerly over them because we ourselves, like Snow White, have
feared our mother's envy; because, like Little Briar Rose, we
imagine the gap between the child and the woman to stretch
over a hundred years; because, like Cinderella, we long to be
protected by the good mother from the bad mother. Seen in this
way, it is clear that fairy tales play a significant part in helping
us grow up – and that they are able to do this because they

introduce us to ideas about change, conflict and coming-to-maturity through the medium of make-believe. A thread that runs through all fairy tales, and is important for our own writing, is the element of change. A world which is wrong, which contains envy and malice, is reordered, made new. The hero or heroine is helped to overcome the destructive aspects of her world and becomes part of a richer, more integrated whole.

If you look through all the short stories you know, I think you'll find that the element of change lies at the bottom of each, like an insistent ground bass. Something always happens and someone always has to deal with (or avoid) what has occurred. The character can meet the change head on, in which case we may feel gratified – or sidestep the new knowledge, try to behave as though everything is the same as before. Either way, the change *sits* there for the reader, fascinating, not to be ignored. Sometimes the most immense changes are given to us in a short story of only a few pages: Chekhov's 'Let Me Sleep' sees an exhausted, brutalised servant-girl murder a baby in six pages; Katherine Mansfield's 'Revelations' sees a woman who longs for freedom and independence rush for security to an unloved but ardent suitor – because everything feels strange at her hairdresser's, where she learns that a tragedy has occurred – in seven pages.

You may object: 'But changes happen in novels, too. Even in poems. Certainly in plays.' Yes, but in the short story, everything is subordinate to the change. It is the change that counts, rather than the characters or the setting. These elements, much more central to the novel, interlock with the transformation, feed into it, determine it even, but they do not overshadow it. Edith Wharton called a volume of her short stories *Crucial Instances* and that is a good way of describing the form. The short story shows us a character at a crucial instant in her life (parallels with the fairy tale emerge here) and traces the effect of that instant upon her.

Your method of narration is likely to be different in a short story. You haven't the time for lengthy character analysis or exquisite evocations of place. These must be done with swift strokes, as if you were drawing a cartoon rather than painting in oil. Imagine your main character. What are the four most significant aspects of his being? Imagine your place. What

58   CREATIVE WRITING

makes it unique? Why does the change have to happen there? It
is the difference between what Jean Piaget calls syncretistic and
analytic vision. Syncretistic vision represents the salient visible
details, the hero's Brylcreemed hair and pocketful of peanuts,
rather than seeking to explain him in terms of his social and
intellectual background. The short story writer will find ways
of *giving* the character by concentrating on details of dress,
facial expression, speech and action, leaving the reader to fill in
the picture for her or himself. If the outline is firm, the reader
will do the rest of the work.

Making changes

Imagine the scenarios for four short stories. You may not wish
to write them all but imagine them nevertheless and draft out
the pattern of the story. Four changes: the crucial details for
each. In this exercise you will prove to yourself that you can
invent something quite new, a change which perhaps connects
with your own life but is seen from the outside, happening to
someone else.

Before you begin, look at the way Katherine Mansfield
sketched the outlines for her last stories.

STORIES FOR MY NEW BOOK

N.Z. *Honesty:* The Doctor, Arnold Cullen and his wife Lydia,
       and Archie the friend.
L.   *Second Violin:* Alexander and his friend in the train.
       Spring . . . wet lilac . . . spouting rain.
N.Z. *Six Years After:* A wife and husband on board a steamer.
       They see someone who reminds them. The cold
       buttons.
L.   *Lives Like Logs of Driftwood:* This wants to be a long,
       very well written story. The men are important,
       especially the lesser man. It wants a great deal of
       working . . . newspaper office.
N.Z. *A Weak Heart:* Roddie on his bike in the evening, with his
       hands in his pockets, *doing marvels* by that dark tree at
       the corner of May Street.

L.   *Widowed:* Geraldine and Jimmie, a house overlooking
      Sloane Street and Square. Wearing those buds at her
      breast. "Married or not married" . . . From autumn to
      spring.

(L. and N.Z. refer to London and New Zealand, the settings for
the stories.)

Katherine Mansfield, *The Collected Short Stories*.

Mansfield thought out her stories first, made brief notes to
remind herself of the details, of the change that was to take
place, and *then* wrote. She wrote in her journal on New Year's
Day 1922:

> Wrote *The Doves' Nest* this afternoon. I was in no mood to
> write; it seemed impossible. Yet, when I had finished three
> pages, they 'were all right!' This is a proof (never to be too
> often proved) that when one has thought out a story nothing
> remains but the *labour*.

There are at least two schools of thought on the way short
stories come to be written. One holds that the writer does most
of the work beforehand, laying a plan that is rather like an egg –
and the story hatches, almost of its own accord. The other holds
that we discover what we have to say through the process of
writing – D. H. Lawrence would support this view. There may
be a middle road, too: one that knows the importance of the
preliminary schema but is not surprised if something new
emerges in the actual writing. If you believe, as I do, that
miracles sometimes take place between the brain and the
writing hand, that we do not always know what we want to
write until we have written it, then you will be gratified when
the unconscious makes one of its surprise and glorious forays
onto the page and not seek to suppress what has been given
without your asking.

6

Speaking in Different Tongues, Different Tones

WE have concentrated up to now on ways of starting to write in our own voice: through calling up early memories, waking up the senses and developing an ear for the rhythms of speech. But what if you have more than one writing voice? (You have.) What if there are several voices inside you, all waiting to be heard? (There are.) If you think about your own personality, you will recognise that even your conscious self is composed of different facets. With one friend you may be the epitome of patient listening, with another the garrulous fool. With a lover you may be tender, or outrageously jealous, and with a child you may be alternately nurturing, supportive and strict, even punitive. Each one of us is many people. Just think of all the people you are at different times, in different places. Think of all the selves you put on – selves that aren't really masks because they are a true part of the core being – but that often coexist uneasily, compelling us to recognise the tension and contradictions between the different selves. If we feel whole, then all these aspects of our being seem to be looped together in a loose, flexible unity. The contradictions remain but they only become tension and conflict when we are under pressure to perform more than one role at a time.

Writers, as I've argued before, tend to use these contradictions rather than try to pretend they're not there. Being a writer is in itself a type of contradiction because it means that you are both an actor, a participant in the world and also an observer, an interpreter, a maker of meaning. In this chapter we will channel our energies into opening up the contradictory facets of our personalities and explore the different voices, different tones of voice, that these contradictions make available to us. The two voices I want us to concentrate on are 'the laughing voice' and 'the Gothic voice'.

The laughing voice

First we have to consider carefully what makes us laugh. Examine all the humour you come across – in shops, at work, with children, on the TV – and try to ascertain what it is that makes something funny for you. You will find the apparently mechanical task of taking jokes and funny situations apart, to see what elements they're composed of, extremely helpful for your own work. Perhaps you're saying 'I can't do that. Cutting it up like a load of old fish.' Don't be afraid of doing this. We don't destroy humour just because we seek to understand it. And we need to understand it so we can produce it ourselves.

Trevor Griffiths asks many painful, searching questions about laughter and humour in his play *The Comedians*. In the unlikely setting of an adult education evening class for would-be comics, a once-famous comedian puts forward his views about what comedy should do. He believes it should take the parts of our lives that are most sore, most hurtful, most unspoken, most taboo and bring them into the public sphere. When these deeply hidden parts of ourselves are spoken out, they produce a feeling of relief in the audience because they have similar wounds, similar fears and that relief often comes out as laughter. Like the Jewish American comedian Joan Rivers, for example, who tells jokes about herself as a Jewish woman that key into other women's silent insecurities. When she was interviewed on the television recently she said things like:

> *Interviewer*: I understand your husband had a heart-attack recently.
> *Joan Rivers*: Yes. Thankfully, he's getting better now. But I gave it to him you know. We were making love, and I took the paper bag off my head.
> *Interviewer*: You have very strong views on women in bed.
> *Joan Rivers*: Yes. To start with, a woman must fake in bed, must fake orgasm. It's common courtesy.

Interviewer: You say you're not happy about your body.
Joan Rivers: Hell no. My thighs are so wobbly. Thank God
my stomach covers them. I said to my husband
the other day 'Say something nice to me. Say
something nice about my legs.' He said 'Blue
goes with everything.'

In simply giving voice to the fears of aging that our society
makes sure women have, Joan Rivers has discovered a rich vein
of comedy. And in turning the fear into laughter by speaking it
out, she is participating in one of comedy's most valuable
functions: that of disrupting the *status quo*. If we can laugh out
loud about getting old, break the silence that surrounds it
instead of suffering quietly, then we are beginning to escape
from a fear society wants us to have – so we will buy uplift bras,
expensive face creams and continue to fear and envy younger
women. By speaking out about envy between women, comedy
can play a part in helping us to heal it in ourselves.

In *The Comedians*, when the once-famous comic tries to
explain the healing power of humour, he has to work against his
students, who keep falling back into racist, sexist jokes, jokes
about cripples, jokes about anyone who is different. They tell
these jokes when they get nervous, because they are easy,
always sure to get a laugh. This is the humour that does not
heal, the sort that encourages hatred of outsiders. It is the
pantomime humour we all grew up with, where the compère
talks about the organist's big organ and his steamed up glasses.
Fundamentally, it is about embarrassment and shame and
keeping us all in our place.

When you consider what makes you laugh, try to distinguish
between the humour that opens things up, that enables you to
confront painful areas and makes you feel stronger, and the
humour that operates at the level of the stock response, works
on your fear, keeps your defences up and makes you feel
weaker. The two types of humour perform opposing functions,
pull in opposite directions. The first type can help to produce
writing of lasting benefit, while the second does nothing but
increase fear and prejudice.

Here is a passage from *The Secret Diary of Adrian Mole*. If it makes you laugh, try to discover where the pleasure comes from.

Sunday April 5th
PASSION SUNDAY

Nigel came round this morning. He is still mad about Pandora. I tried to take his mind off her by talking about the Norwegian leather industry but he couldn't get interested somehow.

I made my father get up at 1 p.m. I don't see why he should lie stinking in bed all day when I am up and about. He got up and went outside to clean the car. He found one of my mother's earrings down the side of the back seat and he just sat there staring at it. He said 'Adrian, do you miss your mother?' I replied, 'Of course I do, but life must go on.' He then said, 'I don't see why.' I took this to mean that he was suicidal, so I immediately went upstairs and removed anything harmful from the bathroom.

After we had eaten our frozen roast-beef dinner and I was washing up, he shouted from the bathroom for his razor. I lied and shouted back that I didn't know where it was. I then removed every knife and sharp instrument from the kitchen drawer. He tried to get his battery razor to work but the batteries had leaked and gone all green.

I like to think I am broad-minded, but the language my father used was beyond the pale, and all because he couldn't have a shave! Tea was a bit of a drag. My grandma kept saying horrible things about my mother and my father kept rambling on about how much he missed her. Nobody even noticed I was in the room! The dog got more attention than me!

My grandma told my father off for growing a beard. She said 'You may think it amusing to look like a communist, George, but I don't.' She said that even in the trenches at Ypres my grandad had shaved every day. Sometimes he had to stop rats from eating his shaving soap. She said that my grandad was even shaved by the undertaker when lying in his coffin, so if the dead could shave there was no excuse for

the living. My father tried to explain, but grandma didn't
stop talking once so it was a bit difficult.
We were both glad when she went home.
Looked at *Big and Bouncy*. It is Passion Sunday after all!

I think that here, Sue Townsend is playing with notions of
expected behaviour. Adrian Mole says and does things we
would not expect from an adolescent. He is up and about before
his father and he gets his father up, as if *he* were the parent and
his father the sleepy child. We don't expect Adrian to say 'life
must go on'. He is stoical and resigned, while his father is
emotional. Adrian becomes the over-protective parent to his
miserable father and although we can understand how this
behaviour comes about in a child whose parents are asserting
their own needs, who are themselves needy children, it
nevertheless feels funny, feels inappropriate. He is a child aping
the conventional responses of an adult. He takes care of his
parents because they can no longer take care of him or of
themselves. Perhaps this accounts for our dual response to the
book: we are simultaneously moved to tears and to laughter.

There is also a tendency to state the obvious in a way that
stops it from being obvious. When Adrian writes 'Nobody even
noticed I was in the room!' with its exclamation mark of
outrage at the end, part of us says 'Of course they didn't notice.
They were too busy arguing about your mother to see you,'
while another part understands and sides with Adrian's
outrage: 'There's no of course about it. How *could* they ignore
you?' The author undermines 'adult' notions of what is normal
and natural and obvious by showing them through the eyes of a
young boy who is trying to puzzle it all out.

Sue Townsend has an eye and an ear for the ridiculous: the
thought of a son putting away all sharp instruments to stop his
father killing himself moves us to laughter. And the
grandmother's homily in all its macabre detail, leading up to
'so if the dead could shave there's no excuse for the living'
releases a humorous response because it seems just what a
respectable parent *would* say, in desperation to whip her errant
son back to the straight 'n' narrow. We recognise the ridiculous
details because they are also a part of our own lives.

I recently heard Alan Bennett talking about the humour in

his plays and he said that he began to develop his ear for the ridiculous simply by listening to members of his family. He remembered sitting in silence with his grandmother as evening drew on ('always in darkness because she had the idea that light was expensive') while she occasionally read out a headline from the newspaper. The darkness would be pierced by statements like 'Pope braves drizzle' and 'I see the President of Rumania's mother's dead. There's allers trouble for somebody.' I am not sure why the idea of an old woman in an unlit room reading out newspaper headlines for her grandson tickles me so, but it does. I think part of it has to do with recognition – I remember listening to my own grandmother's mysterious pronouncements – and part with a renewed sense of the strangeness of it. There is a connection with Joan Rivers here. If she hadn't spoken those secret fears ('I am so ugly. I will surely give someone a heart attack. . . . I have varicose veins in my legs. I must cover them up.') they would remain unexamined, unchallenged. By hearing them, we recognise them and we also, perhaps for the first time, see them as strange. We hear her speak, we hear the other women laughing and we think 'If we all have these fears, why need we be afraid? I am no uglier than anyone else. My ugliness is becoming strange to me.'

The Gothic voice

Our other voice, the Gothic voice, can give us a very different sensation. Comedy can give comfort and security, can make us feel more at home in our skin. Gothic horror does the opposite: it frightens us out of our skin, discomforts us and turns what we think we know into something unreal and daunting. Whereas comedy can enable us to know the world better, stories of mystery and horror insist on all we cannot know and therefore increase our fear of a disordered, malefic universe. Gothic tales are characterised by gloom, the grotesque and the supernatural. In a peculiar way, Gothic tales are related to comedy. They both show us a topsy-turvy world, a world turned inside-out by the particular lens through which it is viewed. But whereas comedy is capable of taking us out of fear, the Gothic tends to take us further in.

Let's begin by naming our own fears. Which of the following frighten you?

birds	being pursued
cats	knowing that someone
	knows your secret
rats	blood
dead bodies	the dark
locked rooms	open spaces
thick curtains	strangers
being watched	strange looking people
being alone	being taken over by someone else
being locked in	what else?

If you're at all like me, your list will be very long. Sometimes, just thinking about fear is enough to start the palms sweating. It would seem that our capacity to feel fear is great and the merest trigger can set it off. So what makes us want to read stories that frighten us? The psychotherapist says 'Look at the wish behind the fear.' Look at the wish to be locked in, the wish for the dark, the wish to be watched, to have one's secrets known, to be taken over by someone else. And look at the way the wish connects with the fear, in a kind of fascinated ambivalence, a horrified curiosity about experiencing, through literature, something we may unconsciously want but by which we are consciously appalled.

When was the first time you were in the dark, locked in and taken over by someone else? Think back, into the dark, the dark places, the place even before conscious memory. The place you had to fight your way out of, shouting and wailing as you first hit the light; the place that imprisoned you, yet kept you warm, fed you. The place where you were not yourself, but an appendage, a parasite on someone else. Think back to the time before you were you. It is impossible with our conscious mind to fully know what we feel about this place but the Gothic tale can set in motion atavistic fears and fantasies. An atavism is a throwback, a 'primitive' reaction (it literally means 'great-grandfather's grandfather') – something the writer must know about in himself if his work is to resonate in his readers.

In 'The Fall of the House of Usher', Edgar Allan Poe invokes the fear of being shut in which he projects into the fear of shutting someone else in. In this case, Madeline Usher has been buried in the family vault below the house, supposedly dead.

It was, especially, upon retiring to bed late in the night of the seventh or eighth day after the placing of the Lady Madeline within the donjon, that I experienced the full power of such feelings. Sleep came not near my couch – while the hours waned and waned away. I struggled to reason off the nervousness which had dominion over me. I endeavoured to believe that much, if not all of what I felt, was due to the bewildering influence of the gloomy furniture in the room – of the dark and tattered draperies, which, tortured into motion by the breath of a rising tempest, swayed fitfully to and fro upon the walls, and rustled uneasily about the decorations of the bed. But my efforts were fruitless. An irrepressible tremor gradually pervaded my frame; and, at length, there sat upon my very heart an incubus of causeless alarm. Shaking this off with a gasp and a struggle, I uplifted myself upon the pillows, and, peering earnestly within the intense darkness of the chamber, hearkened – I know not why, except that an instinctive spirit prompted me – to certain low and indefinite sounds which came, through the pauses of the storm, at long intervals, I knew not whence. Overpowered by an intense sentiment of horror, unaccountable yet unendurable, I threw on my clothes with haste (for I felt that I should sleep no more during the night), and endeavoured to arouse myself from the pitiable condition into which I had fallen, by pacing rapidly to and fro through the apartment.

When we look at Poe's tales, the structure seems predictable, even formulaic: the dawning sense that all is not as it should be; the attempts to explain away the moaning sounds that something inside him is nevertheless compelling him to hear; the fight with fancy, as if one could will away one's deepest fear; and then the horrified recognition that what one was most afraid of is *there*, behind the antique panels, waiting to throw one to the floor. But if all this forms part of a familiar pattern, why are we still afraid when we read it? Perhaps it is because, though we can consciously trace the outline of the fear, it reaches so far into the hidden recesses of our minds that we cannot control the involuntary response. Perhaps it speaks to a part of our mind that does not know about self-control – a part that remembers the time when we were entirely in someone else's power and they, in a certain sense, were in ours.

Poe calls up all these feelings – and leaves us stranded on their shores. One has the sense that he himself was beached there and that one of his comforts lay in writing out his fears in order to bring his readers to the same sands where he lay struggling for air. Poe does not seem to know his way back into the water.

There are stories, however, that *know* the depths of these fears, take their readers into them, into the experience, and then out through the other side. These are the stories that possess the gift of healing. The reader feels, after reading them, as if he/she had followed Theseus into the labyrinth, faced the Minatour and helped to slay the beast, then followed the clew back into the outside world. The reader assists at the triumph over the abyss and experiences, in a very important way, his/her own coming-through or rite of passage. I have said that Poe's tales take the reader to somewhere he/she is not him or herself; these Gothic stories *restore* the reader to him or herself.

One Gothic tale I am thinking of in particular is the Grimm's fairy tale called 'Fitcher's Bird' which is the prototype for all the Bluebeard stories. In it, a wizard enchants two sisters, one after the other, to accompany him to his house in the depth of the forest. They each fall utterly under his spell and promise to obey him in everything, whereupon he tells them that he has to go on a journey and gives them the keys of his magnificent house but forbids them to enter a room which is opened by a particular little key. He also gives each of them an egg to take care of. The first, then the second, sister is overcome by curiosity and enters the bloody chamber.

A great bloody basin stood in the middle of the room, and hard by was a block of wood, and a gleaming axe lay upon it. She was so terribly alarmed that the egg which she held in her hand fell into the basin. She got it out and wiped the blood off, but in vain; it appeared again in a moment. She washed and scrubbed, but she could not get it off.

When the wizard returns he punishes each sister for her curiosity.

He threw her down, dragged her along by her hair, cut her head off on the block, and hewed her in pieces. Then he threw her into the basin. . . .

Then he went and brought the third sister, but she was clever and wily. When he had given her the keys and the egg, and had left her, she first put the egg away with great care, and then examined the house, and at last went into the forbidden room. Alas, what did she behold! Both her dear sisters lay there in the basin, cruelly murdered, and cut in pieces. But she began to gather their limbs together and put them in order, head, body, arms and legs. And when nothing further was wanting the limbs began to move and unite themselves together, and both the maidens opened their eyes and were once more alive. Then they rejoiced and kissed and caressed each other.

The third sister then puts into operation an elaborate plan to get all the wizard's gold and trap him and all his cohorts in his house, to which her brothers then set fire. She vanquishes the wizard by keeping her wits, by resisting his enchantment. She is just as curious as her sisters, but she has the foresight to put the egg safely away before penetrating the forbidden chamber.

Look at the fears/wishes that are called up in 'Fitcher's Bird': the fear of being enchanted, of having one's own will overcome by that of another; the fear of being punished for one's curiosity, one's will-to-know; the fear of being locked forever in the bloody chamber. They hook into our own deepest fantasies. *We* are the wizard's victim, too.

In this way the story is just like one of Poe's: it calls up buried fears. It also calls upon the symbols most likely to draw us in – an egg, keys, blood and gold. These things mean something different to each one of us but they are central to the culture as a whole and central to our knowledge and fantasies about our own bodies. They seem almost magical in themselves and once incorporated in a story they are guaranteed to weave a web to catch and hold us.

I think one of the reasons 'Fitcher's Bird' is at once so

fascinating and so satisfying is that the third sister is not protected from the enchantment. She is just as much under the wizard's spell as the ones who have gone before; her curiosity is as great. She is just cleverer. Her wits, her power to organise the symbols (to put the egg away and put the bodies back together) ensure her final victory. She can use the enchantment, rather than be overcome by it, because a critical, rational, intelligent, witty part of herself retains its distance. In a way she is a model for the writer in you – the writer who needs to experience the passion, the enchantment, yet keep enough control to effectively organise your symbols. You cannot be completely enchanted yourself because it is your job to enchant others. You are the lover who will woo your readers, who will bring them under your power by the words you write.

Now you need to bring a friend or friends in to help you with your writing because it is time now to test out its effect upon other people.

1. Take one or more of the elements of humour you discovered in yourself and use them to write a funny story. Remember the connection between humour and pain and humour and the taboo. Don't be afraid to open up uncharted areas or kick down a few fences. Your task is to write a gift of laughter for your friend.

2. Take your biggest fear, take three or four symbols (for example, a door, an attic, a ring, a knife) that hold significance for you and organise a story around the fear and the symbols. When you consider this organisation, bear in mind Poe's description of the short story as 'a narrative that can be read at one sitting of from half an hour to two hours, that is limited to a certain unique and single effect *to which every detail is subordinate*.' Give it to a friend to read and find out what effect it had.

7

Hold the Tension,
Hold the Energy

So far we have concentrated on taking control of feelings of
humour or fright so you can represent them in a way which will
evoke strong feelings in your readers. Now we need to explore
how to sustain the states of mind you call up.

Sometimes I find that stories and poems lose force and
energy half-way through. A tremendous amount of care and
ardour has gone into the beginning and then the story tails off,
almost as if that initial effort had been too much. This might
happen because the writer is tired, because he or she wants to
get the writing over and done with; but the fundamental reason
seems to be that the writer has broken contact with the feeling
that originally made him or her want to write the story or poem.
If that contact is broken, the words and events become a sort of
empty recitation, an alienated recounting of something that
cannot proclaim its real significance. The gap between words
and experience is already great; at its best, the language
struggles towards a fullness it can never achieve. We often hear
people say 'I can't express how I felt' or 'Words are
inadequate.' These sayings aren't just conscious evasions.
Words are always inadequate. But some get closer to the
feeling, the experience or the thought than others. And the
writer has to keep conjuring the feeling in him or herself, to keep
it *there*, if he/she is to hope to do the same for the readers. In this
chapter we shall work on ways of maintaining the connection
with the feeling that animates, gives life to the story or the
poem.

Let's begin by looking at a well-known poem – William
Blake's 'London'. I believe it is the most powerful poem he ever
wrote and I want to analyse the way in which he maintains the

clenched fist of resistant energy through four rhyming quatrains.

London

I wander through each charter'd street,
Near where the charter'd Thames does flow,
And mark in every face I meet
Marks of weakness, marks of woe.

In every cry of every Man,
In every Infant's cry of fear,
In every voice, in every ban,
The mind-forg'd manacles I hear.

How the Chimney-sweeper's cry
Every black'ning Church appalls;
And the hapless Soldier's sigh
Runs in blood down Palace Walls.

But most through midnight streets I hear
How the youthful Harlot's curse
Blasts the new born Infant's tear,
And blights with plagues the Marriage hearse.

Think first about the repetitions Blake uses: 'charter'd' occurs twice in the first stanza, and 'marks' three times. Why are these words repeated? What part does repetition play in creating a mood of sorrow, of hopelessness? Sometimes, when writing we repeat a word unknowingly and when we read it again we recognise that our pen has slipped back over old ground: we have not found the right word. But here something different is happening. It is as if Blake is taking our hand and compelling us to see what he sees: streets mapped out, chartered, known, possessing no vital life of their own but *owned*; a river that has been forced to fit into this scheme, that is likewise owned, and hence deprived of some intrinsic quality that should belong to rivers. Faces are marked – stained or branded, disfigured. Repeating these words leads the reader to think that the poet sees these things everywhere he looks.

Look at the rhythm of the poem:

⏑ —| —| —| — |
Ĭ wandĕr through eăch charteř'd street

– di dum di dum di dum di dum. It is one of the commonest rhythms to be found but look what it does here. It is the limping walk of someone who has been crippled – the Greek name for it is the 'iamb', which means 'lame man' – people who have been *manacled, marked, banned, chartered*. Not only does the rhythm fit with what the poet is saying, it plays its own central part in creating the mood and meaning of the poem.

In the first stanza, the poet tells us what he sees; in the second, what he hears. Blake is using one sense after the other, as you have learned to do. By doing this, he is able to show different sides of a thought or feeling, building up the sense-impressions that cluster around it. He could have written, 'Every time I walk through London I realise how chained down everybody is, how people make one another suffer, how no one is free from corruption' – and he would have been greeted with our 'Yes, so you think that. So what?' It has no emotional effect upon the reader because it doesn't show how the poet came to these conclusions. And as the aim of a writer is to take the reader with him, we can learn from the way Blake leads us along the path he is taking.

Look at the connections Blake makes in the third and fourth stanzas. The chimney sweep is bound to the church, not only because he cleans the chimneys that pump out the soot that disfigures the church but also because the church preaches a kind of Christianity that can countenance beating, starving and insanely cruel treatment towards chimney sweeps. Soldiers are compelled to fight, to bleed, to die, to safeguard the interest of the Crown and the State – and Blake makes a metaphor out of that connection by having the soldier's sigh run *in blood* down the walls of the palace.

These connections open out – inevitably, it seems – into the most terrible bond, in the fourth stanza: that between the 'holy', respectable institution of marriage and the harsh, exploitative world of prostitution, where bodies are bought and sold. In the last two stanzas, Blake is explaining the *marks of woe* that he sees in the first stanza – but what extraordinary connections to make! Outrageous they seem at first. Surely it is a kind of blasphemy to hold the church responsible for the cruelty and degradation going on around its blackened doors? Surely it is treacherous to blame the palaces of the rich for all

the blood spilt on battlefields? Surely marriage and prostitution
are separate and it insults marriage to infer that they thrive on
one another? These are the astonished questions we ask when
we first read the poem. But when the dust has settled, when we
consider what we know – from reading history, from films, from
our own experience, we realise that though it *is* outrageous the
connections Blake makes are true ones.

Try to remember the things you've learned from this poem
until you do the next exercise when you will have the
opportunity to transform the knowledge into something
uniquely your own. In the *writer's* place in your mind, retain
these key words:

  repetitions
  rhythm
  sense impressions
  new connections

until it is time to do something with them. If you do this, you
will be making your first experiment with Hemingway's 'letting
the well fill up again' before you return to write. Hemingway
claimed that he always stopped writing about noon, when he
knew what was coming next. He then forced himself to get
through the rest of the day without writing, so that the well
would have replenished its juice by the time he took up his
pencil again the next daybreak.

It is to Hemingway's writing I now want us to turn, to a piece
of reportage published in 1935 called 'Who murdered the
Vets?' The Vets in question are war veterans stationed along
the Florida Keys, employed by the United States Government
to build a railway track. They are, Hemingway writes, 'doing
coolie labor for a top wage of $45 a month and they have been
put down on the Florida Keys where they can't make trouble. It
is hurricane months, sure, but if anything comes up, you can
always evacuate them, can't you?' The Vets were not
evacuated when the hurricane struck and Hemingway reports
on the wind and the tidal wave that killed hundreds of them.
What I find fascinating about these eight pages is that they are
sustained by rage – by a controlled yet immense rage against a
government which could allow its veterans to die – and that
Hemingway has the skill to let his anger unroll, rather like one
of the giant waves caused by the hurricane, until his readers are

held afloat upon it. It is this rage which draws us in, which has us participating in Hemingway's feelings before we know it, that makes the piece so powerful. We need to learn and understand how he *composes* his rage, so we can harness similar potencies in our own writing.

The piece begins in an unlikely way – with three direct accusations.

> Whom did they annoy and to whom was their possible presence a political danger?
> Who sent them down to the Florida Keys and left them there in hurricane months?
> Who is responsible for their deaths?

Hemingway seems to have 'gone off on top doh' and fired all his big guns before the battle has even begun. But after this opening blast, in which he makes clear the depth of his anger, the tone is immediately reined in, measured. 'The writer of this article lives a long way from Washington and would not know the answers to these questions.' That itself is something we can take in: his way of surprising the reader, setting up a kind of emotional ambush, by a sudden switch from violent to measured tone. Hemingway takes us through a hurricane which is predicted, which comes very near but finally misses his home. In doing this, he takes us over the ground first, telling us what to expect, what to look for, so that when the hurricane does hit it hits us harder:

> When we reached Lower Matecumbe there were bodies floating in the ferry slip. The brush was all brown as though autumn had come to these islands where there is no autumn but only a more dangerous summer, but that was because the leaves had all been blown away. There was two feet of sand over the highest part of the island where the wind had carried it and all the heavy bridge-building machines were on their sides. The island looked like the abandoned bed of a river where the sea had swept it. The railroad embankment was gone and the men who had cowered behind it and finally, when the water came, clung to the rails, were all gone with it. You could find them face down and face up in the

mangroves. The biggest bunch of the dead were in the tangled, always green but now brown, mangroves behind the tank cars and the water towers. They hung on there, in shelter, until the wind and rising water carried them away. They didn't all let go at once but only when they could hold on no longer. Then further on you found them high in the trees where the water had swept them. You found them everywhere and in the sun all of them were beginning to be too big for their blue jeans and jackets that they could never fill when they were on the bum and hungry.

By this time we feel as if we are Hemingway's companion, hauling out the bodies one by one, so that when he says 'Well you waited a long time to get sick brother. Sixty-seven of them and you get sick at the sixty-eighth', it is as if he is saying it to us over his shoulder as he bends down to examine another body. He is talking directly to us and we *do* feel sick.

What do we learn from this piece of reportage? That we can, must, involve the reader, make the reader participate in the feeling we are trying to represent; and we learn, too, that there are some subjects, like this one, so powerful in themselves that they require the simplest narration when it is time to take the reader to the climax. In one of Brecht's last poems, 'And I always thought', there are the lines

When I say what things are like
Everyone's heart must be torn to shreds.

When we have made contact with the pervading, dominant feeling in a story or poem and *keep* contact with it, then Brecht is right: the simplest words are enough to tear the reader's heart to shreds.

Now try and achieve this yourself. You have witnessed some appalling incident. Those involved are either too distressed, too wounded or too ill-equipped to say what happened and yet it is vital, for the safety of others, that it be brought to public notice. Describe fully what took place, in a way which will arouse the feelings and sympathy of your readers.

Keeping the connections alive

In Blake's poem and Hemingway's reportage, there is a correspondence between the writer's anger and the conditions that evoke it. The anger is an appropriate response to what the writer describes, a public statement about conditions of life or death. They each address themselves to the reader's understanding of what a just society should be like: they are publicly political writings.

But how do we sustain, in prose or verse, a feeling that is intensely personal, not obviously called up by something 'on the outside' but which seems to be embedded deep within us? Like jealousy, for example?

I think for every feeling, no matter how inward and personal it appears, the writer has to find something in the visible world which corresponds to it, to make it visible for the reader. A feeling has no colour, no outline, no substance of its own. The writer has to give it these things to make it real for the reader.

The things in the 'outside world' which we use to embody or give a shape to our feelings are our metaphors. A dull, cold, rainy day does not literally mean 'sadness' – it is possible to be happy on such a day – but it is so obviously a metaphor for sadness that when it appears in writing it has become a cliché, intended to trigger a predictable response. What we see, or what a character in a story sees, is determined by the frame of mind in which it is seen. When we think of narrative or verse in this way, the underlying feeling assumes a primary importance. So how would we find an outside correspondence for jealousy, a way of writing about it that would make it real for the reader, so real that it puts him/her in touch with his/her own jealousy? To explore this problem, I'm going to talk about two short novels that have jealousy as their central, dominant feeling but are in all other respects wholly different from one another. The first is *Ten-Thirty on a Summer Night* by the French novelist Marguerite Duras, published in 1962.

This novel is about Maria, Pierre and Judith, their child, who are on holiday in Spain with Claire, their young friend. There have been several bad storms on the road and they have decided to break their journey to Madrid and stay overnight in a small town. Maria, a very heavy drinker, has begun to notice signs of passion between Claire and her husband:

> Pierre's hands moved towards hers and then pulled back. Earlier he had made the same gesture, in the car when she was afraid of the storm, the sky rolling over on itself, hanging over the wheatfields.

Though the whole story is written from Maria's viewpoint, no mention is ever made of her jealousy. Pierre's hands are there and what they want to do, and the storm, but not Maria's jealousy. It is enough that we see these things and sit with her while she drinks manzanilla or brandy to wash the sight away (though we are never told why she drinks) – these things are enough to make us participate in what we surmise she must be feeling.

When they all arrive at the small town, police patrols swirl around. The place is electric with drama, with something weighty, weighted down more by the pressure of the storm. A man called Rodrigo Paestra has discovered his nineteen-year-old wife with a lover and shot them both. They are lying in a makeshift morgue, wrapped in brown blankets, and he is still at large. Maria learns from the men she drinks with in the cafe that he is hiding on the rooftops. So – the magnitude of Maria's feelings is given to us because Duras has come up with another jealous person, whose jealousy was great enough to provoke him to murder.

That night, Maria cannot sleep in the hotel. She is preoccupied with the chimney opposite her balcony, against which a shape is leaning. It looks like a man wrapped in a shroud. It is Rodrigo Paestra. She calls to him, again and again. He doesn't answer.

> She wasn't calling any more. He knew it. Again she opened the corridor door. She saw, she could see them, the others, sleeping cruelly separated. She looked at them for a long time. It hadn't been fulfilled yet, this love. What patience, what patience. She didn't leave the balcony. Rodrigo Paestra knew that she was there. He was still breathing, he existed in this dying night. He was there, in the same place, geographically related to her.

As often happens in summer, a climatic miracle occurred. The fog had disappeared from the horizon and then little by little from the whole sky. The storm dissolved. It no longer existed. Stars, yes stars, in the pre-dawn sky. Such a long time. The stars could make you cry.

Maria wasn't calling any more. She wasn't shouting insults any longer. She hadn't called him ever since she had insulted him. But she stayed on this balcony, her eyes on him, on this shape which fear had reduced to animal idiocy. Her own shape as well.

Her own shape as well. By this tiny brushstroke and by the sky which has suddenly cleared, Duras draws the line of connection between Maria and Rodrigo Paestra. Maria confronts and explores her own jealousy through her obsession with the fugitive on the rooftops. She rescues him, drives him out of town as dawn starts to break and leaves him in a wheatfield. She promises to come for him at noon. When she returns to Pierre and Claire, they are unwilling to believe what she claims has happened but they drive with her back to the field and Maria finds the opening in the wheat where he is lying. She is overcome with tenderness towards him, believing him to be asleep. But he is dead. The revolver lies beside him. Pierre comes over and sees him also. Maria and Pierre are the only ones who see him.

Rodrigo Paestra gives a body to the jealousy that lies between Maria and Pierre. In looking at him, Maria sees an aspect of herself, Pierre sees the outcome of the jealousy – a death – and the reader witnesses an internal struggle that has found a public stage. Rodrigo, the storm, the clear night sky, the overwhelming heat in the wheatfield, offer Maria's jealousy dramatic correspondences in the world outside. We read her state of mind from the people, the action and the weather of the story.

That's one way of doing it. Another, far more ambiguous and strange way, can be found in Alain Robbe-Grillet's *Jealousy*. Its title in French, *La Jalousie*, means both jealousy and window shutter or blind; so from the outset the reader is taken into a maze of contending meanings. Is the novel about jealousy or about objects? We never really know. We have a narrator who presents us with a plan of his house, obsessively describes the objects therein and the way his wife, always referred to as A. . . ., moves about the rooms and onto the veranda. Also present, sometimes, is Franck, a neighbouring farmer, who comes at cocktail hour to drink with A. . . . and the narrator. Are Franck and A. . . . having an affair under the narrator's nose? To a readership schooled in *ménages* from *Anna Karenina* to *Dynasty* it would seem so and yet we are never really sure. We know no more than the narrator, within whose obsessively observant mind we wander, searching, like him, for some sure knowledge. Objects assume an immense importance. They change size. Nothing can be taken for granted. The narrator, like Maria in Duras' novel, reveals nothing directly about the feeling of jealousy. The feeling is represented through his perception of objects, through the way he sees the outside world. So, the jealousy does not form a subject of his thought, one among many, but a lens which filters, colours, interprets everything in its own way.

It was A. . . . who arranged the chairs this evening, when she had them brought out on the veranda. The one she invited Franck to sit in and her own are side by side against the wall of the house – backs against this wall, of course – beneath the office window. So that Franck's chair is on her left, and on her right – but further forward – the little table where the bottles are. The two other chairs are placed on the other side of this table, still farther to the right, so that they do not block the view of the first two through the balustrade of the veranda. For the same reason these last two chairs are not turned to face the rest of the group: they have been set at an angle, obliquely oriented towards the open-work balustrade and the hillside opposite. This arrangement obliges anyone sitting there to turn his head around sharply towards the left if he wants to see A. . . . – especially anyone in the fourth chair, which is the farthest away.

The third, which is a folding chair made of canvas stretched on a metal frame, occupies a distinctly retired position between the fourth chair and the table. But it is this chair, less comfortable, which has remained empty.

Although the tone of the narrative seems neutral, empty of feeling, the minute observation of the way A. . . . positions the chairs gradually fills it up, so that it begins to pulsate with energy from a subject that is never once mentioned. It is the correspondences that summon forth the jealousy and hold it, throughout the novel, under the reader's gaze, as we witness the perceptions of a mind pulled awry by the pressure of an overwhelming suspicion. Jealousy is called the green-eyed monster: it affects what is seen.

I'm inclined to think that every dominant feeling in a story or a poem affects what is seen and needs to find its correspondences in events and objects outside, which in their turn make the feeling real to the reader. Every feeling has to find the metaphor(s) which will give it a body.

Now is your opportunity to test out the ideas I have put forward in this chapter. First choose a state of mind, a feeling that you know particularly well. Think yourself into it and *hold* it for a while. How does this feeling affect you? How do you see things when you feel this way? In what ways is this different to your other states of mind and being? What could happen when you are feeling this way? What could *possibly* happen?

1. A story is emerging. Write it.
2. A poem is coming into focus. Write it.

8

Developing your Narrative

WE now come to the question of the long narrative, the novel, and how we can approach the writing of one. I must admit this is the fence I do not want to jump, for though I know there are new novels that succeed, I am at something of a loss to describe, in reasonable critical terms, *why* they succeed. The novels that have moved me most (Tillie Olsen's *Yonnondio*, F. M. Mayor's *The Rector's Daughter*, Alice Walker's *The Colour Purple*) leave me with the impression that a miracle has happened – a 'How could it be done? Oh! She has done it.' I am surprised whenever a good novel comes to be written because I understand the odds it was written against.

If we think of the great 19th-century novels, published at a time when the novel as a form was still new, but confident, secure in its legitimacy as a writing form, we know that *that* kind of novel could not be written today. In narratives as diverse as *Jane Eyre* and *Great Expectations*, we are aware, when reading, of a certain inevitability of outcome: the writer has us by the hand – *in* his or her hand, almost – and we know we will be led, not necessarily to a happy conclusion but that the narrative will be resolved at a place that feels safe and right, that leaves us satisfied. We know we have been reading a novel but nevertheless we can believe that what the author has told us is true. Perhaps not the literal truth (it is unlikely that Jane Eyre, the unloved orphan, should come into a fortune and gain mastery over Rochester who was once her master or that Pip should be 'raised from his station' by a mysterious benefactor, who turns out to be Magwich, the convict he once fed), but what Henry James called 'the truth of the imagination'.

Dickens's genius lies in his ability to show, in his novels, the social connections which would otherwise have remained buried. In the lawyer Jaggers' office, Pip sees the death-mask of Estelle's mother, a murderess. He has to recognise that this young woman, his object of adoration, was born to a mother who had been driven to murder. He has to recognise that his own mysteriously-found wealth comes from Magwich, who, after his transportation, made a small fortune in Australia. The respectable rich are compelled to look at the origins of their wealth, and at their own origins, which lie in crime, exploitation – in the unseen, unmentioned parts of Victorian society. Dickens manages to see life steadily and see it whole.

How can that be done now?

Remember that Dickens was writing before Freud had begun to uncover the immense complexity of the human personality, before William James's pioneering work on consciousness, which showed that our conscious mind is not solid but that it runs like a stream, swirling endlessly around symbols, associations from the past; always moving, never at rest. Dickens was writing before Marcel Proust and James Joyce, in their different ways, represented this endless swirling in fiction. Before the First World War, which slaughtered a whole generation of men. Before the Great Depression, which shook so fundamentally any belief in the possibility of continuous economic growth. Before Auschwitz, which shattered any previous, optimistic belief about human nature. After all of this, how can the novelist still see life steadily, still see it whole?

For Virginia Woolf, it was the First World War that *broke* something undefinable, something precious, in social intercourse:

Before the war at a luncheon party like this people would have said precisely the same things but they would have sounded different, because in those days they were accompanied by a sort of humming noise, not articulate, but musical, exciting, which changed the value of the words themselves . . . .
Shall we lay the blame on the war? When the guns fired in August 1914, did the faces of men and women show so plain in each other's eyes that romance was killed? Certainly it was a shock (to women in particular with their illusions about education, and so on) to see the faces of our rulers in the light

of the shell-fire. So ugly they looked – German, English,
French – so stupid. But lay the blame where one will, on
whom one will, the illusion which inspired Tennyson and
Christina Rosetti to sing so passionately about the coming of
their loves is far rarer now than then. One has only to read, to
look, to listen, to remember.

A Room of One's Own

A writer must face the terrifying complexity of contemporary
life if her fictions or poems are to be relevant to the world today.
That means keeping one's ears and eyes open, it means not
looking away but acting as a *witness*. But how, you may object,
does one begin?

Proceed from the bits and pieces

Yeats writes:

> I must lie down where all the ladders start:
> In the foul rag-and-bone shop of the heart.

The poet H.D. (Hilda Dolittle) writes:

> I go to where I am loved
> into the snow
> with no thought
> of love or duty.

Adrienne Rich writes:

> If you can read and understand this poem
> send something back: a burning strand of hair
> a still-warm, still-liquid drop of blood
> a shell
> thickened from being battered year on year
> send something back.

The writer-self tunnels back into the foul rag-and-bone shop of
the heart, into the lumber room, dark and sometimes

frightening, where memory dwells. Memory is not abstract. It is made of bits and pieces, sometimes called junk. These are your materials, the things you begin with. You take them out to another place, into the snow, where the light is winter-bright and you can see very clearly. In this light the junk undergoes a transfiguration. It shines, it becomes something very precious, a gift you touch, caress and give back to your reader: something worth having. Writing is your imagination's rescue work. Is there anything too vile to bring out into the light? No. When it is aired it looks and feels different. It has a use. Not just for you – because writing is never *merely* therapeutic, though a healing does occur – but for your readers too.

So, at the start of Tillie Olsen's *Yonnondio*:

> The whistles always woke Mazie. They pierced into her sleep like some gutteral-voiced metal beast, tearing at her; breathing a terror. During the day if the whistle blew, she knew it meant death – somebody's poppa or brother, perhaps her own – in that fearsome place below the ground, the mine.
>
> "God damn that blowhorn," she heard her father mutter. Creak of him getting out of bed. The door closed, with yellow light from the kerosene lamp making a long crack on the floor. Clatter of dishes. Her mother's tired, grimy voice.

I don't know whether Tillie Olsen lived near a mine in her childhood. Perhaps she did or perhaps the mine is a gathering-together of memories – of being shut in, starved of air, of light, of freedom of mind and body. It has a physical reality at the same time as a metaphorical reality. Perhaps she started from the feeling and then found a correspondence for it in the outside world. At all events, it enables her to explore the *danger* that shoots through many childhoods: the fear of losing mother or father, the conflict we often endure as we hear their exasperated voices arguing above our heads or while we are in bed.

Gabriel Garcia Marquez' *A Hundred Years of Solitude* also begins with a childhood but it engages with a quite different feeling:

Many years later, as he faced the firing squad, Colonel Aureliano Buendía was to remember that distant afternoon when his father took him to discover ice. Macondo was a village of twenty adobe houses, built on the bank of a river of clear water that ran along a bed of polished stones, which were white and enormous, like prehistoric eggs. The world was so recent that many things lacked names, and in order to indicate them it was necessary to point. Every year during the month of March a family of ragged gypsies would set up their tents near the village, and with a great uproar of pipes and kettledrums they would display new inventions. First they brought the magnet. A heavy gypsy with an untamed beard and sparrow hands, who introduced himself as Melquíades, put on a bold public demonstration of what he himself called the eighth wonder of the learned alchemists of Macedonia. He went from house to house dragging two metal ingots and everybody was amazed to see pots, pans, tongs and braziers tumble down from their places and beams creak from the desperation of nails and screws trying to emerge, and even objects that had been lost for a long time appeared from where they had been searched for most and went dragging along in turbulent confusion behind Melquíades' magical irons. 'Things have a life of their own,' proclaimed the gypsy with a harsh accent. 'It's simply a matter of waking up their souls.'

Tillie Olsen's novel begins with the whistle breaking into Mazie's sleep and Marquez's with the firing-squad, ice and magnets. It is as if each writer had taken the memory of some powerful event (the terrible shock of being woken by a piercing noise; discovering the 'magical' properties of magnets) and daydreamed in such a concentrated way about it that a group of people, a situation, a story began to emerge. The story may, when it is 'out', bear only a passing resemblance to the writer's own life (although Marquez, at least, has admitted that his novel is firmly grounded in memories of his own childhood) because of the transforming power of the daydream. But it is the memory that sits like a kernel at the heart of it all.

In *A Hundred Years of Solitude* we even sense that the writer wants to take us back into childhood, into the time when 'the world was . . . recent.' The world *is* recent at the dawn of human history and also at the start of a child's life because at both times it is perceived by new eyes. At both times things lack names and it is necessary to point. At both times we see the world with a clarity that we later lose. By conflating childhood with mythic time – and does not the world possess mythic proportions when we are small? Are not adults figures of great power, who can help us grow or else destroy us? Are they not gods, to the child? – the writer enables the reader to go back, to see again what we once saw, but this time with the eyes of an adult, the adult who *regards* the child in herself.

Daydreams and their purposes

In *The Interpretation of Dreams*, Sigmund Freud had this to say about daydreams:

> Like dreams, they are wish-fulfilments; like dreams, they are based to a great extent on impressions of infantile experiences; like dreams, they benefit by a certain degree of *relaxation of censorship*. If we examine their structure, we shall perceive the way in which the wishful purpose that is at work has *mixed up the material* of which they are built, has rearranged it and formed it into *a new whole*. They stand in much the same relation to the childhood memories from which they are derived as do some of the *Baroque palaces* of Rome to the ancient ruins whose pavements and columns have provided the material for more recent structures.
>
> (my italics)

I cannot emphasise enough the importance of daydreams for the writer in you. They occupy the time that *seems* vacant, as if you were just hanging around doing nothing – but where in reality the well is filling up, where you are gathering together the material that will make up your narrative; rearranging it, transforming it. What Freud called the *wishful purpose* could also be called the *structuring principle*. It is able to build a palace out of a ruin; it is the shaping spirit of your narrative.

In this chapter we've been looking at two novels which,.

though they both contain their own particular stylistic innovations, nevertheless stick to the recognised, traditional shape of the novel. They look like any other novel if you just flick over the pages and they are divided into chapters. But what if *your* wishful purpose is not taking you in this direction? Well, fortunately, new ground has been broken by some of our novelists, ground which can be husbanded by new writers. Publishers now accept novels which are composed of a series of short, interlinked stories, novels where prose narrative alternates with poems and – perhaps most interestingly – the epistolary novel has been resurrected, along with the novel of fragments, where every page contains a separate 'statement' that is linked to every other statement through place, character and feeling. Alice Walker's *The Colour Purple* is an example of the first and Monique Wittig's *The Lesbian Body* of the second.

You are standing on the edge now. You know what can be done in a novel. You have examined the work of other authors, which I called to your attention only to indicate the avenues that are open to us, not to say 'This is great writing: emulate it.' I don't know what great writing is. I only know what moves me. You now know, to some degree, what moves you and gives you pleasure. You have found things from your past that you can use. You know the power of the daydream to transform the lumber-room's contents into precious jewels. Lie down. Roll your eyes back to slow your mind down.

Open the door of the lumber-room. The air is thick with dust, accumulated over years of not-remembering, years of not wanting to know. You can hardly breathe at first. You are afraid and full of excitement at thoughts of what you might find. You feel around in the dark. There is only a tiny crack of light under the door. Not enough to see by. You stumble. Your foot has encountered something hard/something soft/something wet/something dry. You reach down, feel it, lift it up gently. You do not know what it is. All you know is that you want it. It is the fragment that will lie at the heart of your novel. You carry it out into the white, shimmering light. You look at it, wonderingly.

What is it? What, or whom, does it call to mind? Whom does it summon forth? They are coming, all of them. There is a company of characters drawn to the object. Who are they?

What is their connection to one another? They are talking. What do they say? The object somehow binds them all together. It possesses a history, a knowledge. What is this knowledge? Their eyes are wide open as they pass the object round. It means something different to each of them and they are all astonished. Why? What is the drama? When did it happen? What started it, or who?

You are utterly prepared for this and utterly ignorant. The writing work you've done as you followed the course of this book has laid the foundations for the palace you're about to build. You opened the door of memory early on, engaged with your early fears, your early triumphs. You learned the potency of place, the joy of movement, the way each sense participates in the pleasure of writing. You taught your people to speak, you learned about the shape of stories. You learned to keep the feeling high, to communicate with the energy of your reader. All this will help you.

But there is a sense in which it won't. This, this novel, this *place* you are going to inhabit, is unknown, uncharted, to anyone except you. *And you have forgotten the way.* You are sure you knew it once but now it is so hazy. Will you lose yourself? What will you discover? You need a map.

Make a map. Draw the shape of your novel. Name your people and make clear to yourself how they are connected. Draw in the events, make a chart of how they build to the climax. Name to yourself the climax, so you know what you are writing towards. The map may prove to be inadequate. You may find a stream, a cave, a factory, a prison you did not know was there but which insists upon itself as a landmark. No matter. You need a map to start with, if only for security, like a childhood blanket or toy weapon. Make a map. Now discover the name of the country. Where is this novel happening?

Now you are beginning your novel.

9

Reaching an Audience

THE writer occupies a split world. One part, the part that writes, that creates something new, requires a protected private space, a 'dark backward abysm' out of which daydreams can be called up in security. The other part, the part that needs to communicate, to reach an audience, knows that it is necessary to come out of that darkly private place, to present one's writing in public, to gauge the responses of a listening group.

A good way of starting to do this is to either join an already-existent writing class (you can find one by looking on the noticeboard in your local library, telephoning the local Further, Adult or Higher Education Centre or contacting the nearest Workers' Educational Association) or, if there isn't one of these in your area, by forming your own writing group. This is your way of coming out of the closet as a writer.

There are various summer writing courses in Britain and America. They can last for anything between a weekend and three weeks and they involve journeying to a place (sometimes a large house has been rented for the time; sometimes a college) where you will eat, talk, be taught, sleep, *live* writing in a totally concentrated way for the length of the course. They are usually organised by well-established foundations (the Arvon Foundation, for example) and they offer you the opportunity of working with and learning from well-known writers.

Avoid the impulse to sneer at writing courses. Many people cut themselves off from great sources of nourishment and direction because they imagine that writing cannot be taught, or if it can, that you can't learn about it in a group. That attitude is perhaps more prevalent in Britain than in America. Remember that many of out best writers now teach as well as write (perhaps to supplement the income they earn from royalties, but also because they simply want and like to) and that you can learn a great deal from the writers you admire. Sylvia Plath and Anne Sexton both attended Robert Lowell's writing class, and Lowell himself camped on Allen Tate's lawn so he could be with him and learn what one experienced poet could teach a younger one.

Surveying the market

When you've reached the point where you *want* publication, where seeing your work in print is necessary to you in order to feel you've made a permanent communication – then you have to begin the work of looking at the market, seeing what is published and by whom.

Haunt your local libraries and bookshops. Scrutinise the fiction and poetry being published this year. Can you see a pattern emerging? Can you see the kinds of books a particular publisher tends to market? Use your notebook here. Take one publisher at a time and look at this year's list. What is each one interested in? Can you discern an editorial leaning or tendency in the work they accept? One might be interested in modernist writing and another in science fiction, for example.

Take a good look at the *Writers' and Artists' Yearbook*, which lists the publishers of all the books on the library shelves, plus some you may not have come across yet. There are some, quite small publishers who are particularly open to new work. Find who they are, then ask your library to get some of their books for you. Remember that you are a business person now, thorough and tenacious, determined to discover the best possible outlets for your work. In the *Yearbook* you will also find a list of small magazines which publish poems, stories and (sometimes) parts of plays. It will not list them all because small magazines come and go, flourish for a while then 'die, that poetry may live', as Gertrude Stein said. Some of these will be on the periodical shelves at your library and others you might want to send off for. It is in the pages of these magazines that I think we can see most clearly how editorial policy, whether it is conscious or unconscious on the part of the editors, operates.

As you begin to send your work around to the various publications, keep a record of which stories and poems have gone where. Be prepared for many, many rejection slips. The American poet Marianne Moore said that she had sometimes to send a piece of work to forty different magazines before it was finally accepted. You may feel depressed when your work is returned to you, feel a failure, but magazine editors reject work for lots of different reasons not all connected with the quality of the work. Perhaps they did not like what you were saying – it didn't fit in with the way they see their magazine. Perhaps the magaine is full for the next three issues and they don't want to commit themselves any further ahead. If you sent your work to a publisher and have not heard from them for two months, you should write to ask them whether or not they intend to publish it. Remember that many editors produce their magazine with little or no subsidy, so they are, in effect, doing the work for love. Bear this in mind when you feel impatient or impolite.

Competitions

Literary competitions abound now. Some are local, some national and their prizes range from £10 to £5000. If you decide to enter a competition, be sure to find out first who the judges are and read some of their work. Not to imitate it, of course, but to gauge whether any of them are likely to be interested in the kind of work you write. If you don't think they will be, you can enter the competition anyway but not waste any energy on hoping for an award.

If you have entered many competitions and never won a thing, this might not be because your work is poor. Remember that the main judges don't see the bulk of the entries because the competition organisers weed them out beforehand. In a sense, the competition is judged even before it is judged. Philip Larkin, in his book *Required Writing*, tells a peculiar story about judging a poetry competition where there were no love poems or nature poems. He asked the organisers 'Where are the love and nature poems?' and they replied 'Oh, we weeded them out.' So you might have entered a wonderful poem to that competition and Philip Larkin never got a chance to look at it.

I think competitions can be fun as long as you don't take them at all seriously. They are a lottery but they probably waste less of your money than gambling on horses, and, as vices go, will not wreck your health as smoking or alcohol will.

Getting a novel published

Once you have seen which publishers might be interested in your novel, you begin the long process of sending it to one after another. Send it to one at a time and be prepared to wait a good while for a reply. Write to jog them along after three months. Again, do not be dismayed by rejections. The work of a new writer is always difficult to place. You have no reputation to encourage a publisher; they don't know what to expect. Liza Alther's bestselling novel *Kinflicks* was rejected at least fifty times before it found a home, but when it did it earned her enough money to enable her to devote herself full-time to writing.

If you are able to find a literary agent who will take on your work, the process of having it looked at by publishers will be speeded up for you. You will find a list of literary agents in the Central London Yellow Pages, but some work outside London, too.

To approach one, write, giving an outline of the novel, asking if they would be interested in reading it. If they say no, it might not be because they don't like the sound of it but because their lists are already full and they are unable to take on any more. Alternatively, they may say why they don't like it – bitter, but still useful. Once a literary agent has accepted your work, you stand a better chance of getting it published, though this is still not guaranteed. The agent will send it around to publishing houses where she or he will have contacts, so your work will be seen more quickly and with a more benevolent eye. If and when it is accepted, the agent will take ten per cent commission on your royalties. Also, the *agent* will deal with the rejection slips, not you.

Self-publication

The publishing world is not always ready for new writers. André Gide self-published his first novel with disastrous results (he took most of the copies, unsold, to the shredders) – and Anaïs Nin typeset, printed and sold *Winter of Artifice* herself. If she had not done so, her work might never have been discovered by American readers. The American publishing world was not ready for her but her readership was. At this moment, groups of people are getting together to publish their own work. They might have been refused by mainstream publishers or alternatively, and this is the more likely, they are making a positive choice to do it this way, since self-publication means that the writers can determine exactly what goes into their printed work.

A possible scenario for self-publishers is this: You have been meeting with other writers for some time. You enjoy each other's work. 'Perhaps we could make a performance?' one of you suggests. You hire a room above a pub or in a community centre and hand out invitations to all your friends. You advertise it in libraries, schools and local newspapers and find yourself reading to an audience of about thirty five. You have a lovely time. You make people laugh. You can tell they like it because they tell you so. 'Why don't you make a pamphlet of all this work? I would like to read it,' says someone. You like the idea. You want to find out how you can do it.

There are quicker ways and slower ways but they are all hefty consumers of time. Be prepared for this. Let us say, though, that you simply want to see the work in print. As long as it has a cover and is held together by staples, that's alright with you. So: you type it out on an electric typewriter on A4 or A5 size paper. You arrange the material into the order you want and have it photocopied, preferably using a photocopier that does the collating for you. If you have to do the collating yourself, lay each separate page-pile next to each other around the room and go round picking up one page after the other, until you have the whole pamphlet together. This is much faster and more fun if a group of you do it together. You design a cover, back and front, and choose a title. Then you photocopy that. You staple it all together. And try to sell it. With luck, you might cover your costs but don't count on it. There are many mouldering, unsold pamphlets in people's lofts.

Whether or not this small-scale self-publication works in terms of sales is less important than the extraordinary experience it can provide: that of working hard with a few other writers at making something, putting something into print. The tasks themselves – typing, photocopying, collating, stapling – are not intrinsically interesting but doing them with others, who are eager for the same goal, is.

Unless you have a lot of money you will need to think about the price of all this: you will need to cost your enterprise. What is involved? List all your materials, every part of the process that will cost money and find out beforehand what the cost will be. How many pamphlets do you want to produce? How many can you realistically hope to sell? Will the local bookshops take them on a sale-or-return basis? Remember that booksellers take 33 per cent of your cover price as commission. Distribution is often the small publisher's main headache, so canvas your possible outlets beforehand.

The more ambitious you are for how the magazine is to look, the more time-consuming and expensive your enterprise becomes. You will be looking for a typesetter, help with layout, so the magazine is designed as eye-catchingly as possible, and a printer. If you publish more copies than you can hope to sell yourselves, you may need a distributor. Much planning and forethought is needed before you embark on such a large project. I recommend that you read Gail Chester's *Rolling Our Own*, which explores the work and achievements of women self-publishers, or attend one of her Do-It-Yourself Publishing classes. You should also make contact with the Federation of Worker Writers and Community Publishers.

Useful addresses

You can contact the Federation of Worker Writers at 61, Bloom Street, Manchester, M1 3LY.

The Arts Council Poetry Library publishes lists of poetry magazines (which often also publish short stories), lists of poetry and short story competitions, bookshops which stock poetry magazines and part-time day and evening classes in creative writing. The address is:

Arts Council Poetry Library,
105 Piccadilly,
London W1V 0AU.
Tel. 01–629 9495

Your future

What will happen now? You have begun. Indeed, if you have followed through all the exercises in this book, you have done a substantial amount of work. How will you keep going? Will you be encouraged, or disappointed? It is my belief that any writer, who takes their work seriously, makes it a priority and does not give up, will eventually win a measure of recognition. But how do we not give up? If our work meets with rejection letters and silence on all sides, will we ourselves, in the end, be silenced?

Writer, if you are ever in danger of losing your tongue, read *Silences*. Tillie Olsen can warn you about all the ways it can possibly happen, and show, too, how the best writers have gone quiet in response to discouragement and lack of understanding. Once you know the ways of the enemy, silence, you will be better armed for fighting it. Make yourself a present of *Silences* and keep it by you as a reference book. It is as useful as a dictionary.

The other thing to remember is that when you are caught in that fearful quiet, that sense of the hopelessness of ever writing again, then *any* commission, any writing task set by another person, is a lifesaver. Writing (reviews, letters, short articles, jingles – it is almost immaterial) always improves your writing, always cajoles the writing voice into life again, when it had seemed dead. Don't refuse any writing work that comes your way, even though at first it might not seem to coincide with what you want to write. Writing feeds writing. The more you write, the more you have to write and the stronger your writing voice will become.